LATINO HOMICIDE

LATINO HOMICIDE

Immigration, Violence, and Community

RAMIRO MARTINEZ, JR.

8 RKUSA

Routledge
Taylor & Francis Group

NEW YORK AND LONDON

Published in 2002 by
Routledge
29 West 35th Street
New York, NY 10001
www.routledge-ny.com

Published in Great Britain by
Routledge
11 New Fetter Lane
London EC4P 4EE
www.routledge.co.uk

Routledge is an imprint of the Taylor & Francis Group.

Printed in the United States of America on acid-free paper.

10 9 8 7 6 5 4 3 2 1

Library of Congress Cataloging-in-Publication Data
Martinez, Ramiro.
    Latino homicide : immigration, violence, and community / Ramiro
Martinez, Jr.
        p.   cm.
    ISBN 0-415-93402-8 (hard : alk. paper) — ISBN 0-415-93403-6
(pbk. : alk. paper)
    1. Homicide—United States—Case studies. 2. Latin Americans—
United States—Case studies. 3. Hispanic Americans—Case studies.
4. United States—Emigration and immigration—Case studies.
I. Title.
    HV6529 .M37 2002
    364.15'2'08968073—dc21

2002004516

CRIME, LAW, AND DEVIANCE

Series Editor, John Hagan, Northwestern University

The new *Crime, Law, and Deviance* series publishes high quality books of interest to students and scholars in sociology, law, criminology, criminal justice and related fields. This series is concerned with the developmental processes that lead to deviant behavior, the definitial processes that convert behavior into crime, and the role of law in stimulating, stigmatizing, and sanctioning behavior called criminal. *Latino Homicide: Immigration, Violence, and Community* by Ramiro Martinez, Jr. is the first book in this series.

CONTENTS

TABLES AND FIGURES

TABLES

FIGURES

ACKNOWLEDGMENTS

THIS BOOK is the result of a process that started several years ago. I asked Ruth Peterson, a former professor of mine, a question about Latino youth homicides while in graduate school at Ohio State University. At the time homicide figured prominently in the public health and criminological domain and was a leading cause of death for African-American males. It was difficult to find a similar statistic for Latino homicides. Few knew the extent of criminal homicides for Latino youths or adults. Some federal documents reported figures at the state level in the South and the Southwest, but relatively few violence researchers were paying attention to a large and visible ethnic group. This book was unknowingly started at that moment.

I never knew that my struggle to find answers to apparently simple questions would cost so much—not only in time and money, but also in terms of grappling with issues of crime, violence, race, ethnicity, and immigration. These are potentially explosive topics, and I fear that some of my findings might fuel some stereotypes, but my main hope is that they will destroy others. In fact, I stress that this book is not an "us" versus "them" diatribe and certainly never argue that Latinos are "better" or "worse" than other ethnic groups. Ultimately my primary goal is to ask and answer simple questions about Latinos and homicide, and I hope that my efforts lead to another set of issues that takes others' time and effort to address in the future, using my findings as a springboard for further inquiry on Latinos and crime.

Many people contributed to this project. John Laub and Luis Falcon challenged me during a faculty colloquium at Northeastern University to seek data at the local level. James Inciardi helped me access information in Miami with the help of Marion Kiley. Former city of Miami Police Department (MPD) chief Donald Warshaw and former assistant chief John E. Brooks allowed me to enter the doors on 400 N.W. Second Avenue. Lt. Bobbie Meeks, Lt. John Campbell, and Lt. George Cadavid held them open, and many others in the Homicide Investigations Unit generously showed me where the homicide reports were stored. I would like to thank them and various investigators, staff, and other personnel in the MPD. My thanks to Danny Dominguez, George Law, Devery C. Thumann, Moises Velazquez, Jorge L. Gonzales, Torrance Gary, Veronica J. Allen, Bobby Cheatham, William Schwartz, Richard Cosner, A. J. Johnson, Al Cotera, Oscar Tejeda, Orlando Villaverde, William O'Connor, Willie Everett, Eunice Cooper, Mallory Frank Shonberger, and especially Diego B. Ochoa. Special thanks to Joel Gonzalez, Nelson Andreu, Manny de la Torriente, Al Gardner, Eddie Martinez, Frank Castillo, Frank Alfonso, and Confesor Gonzalez, who opened their homes to me and who took scarce free time from their families to show me the city. Even though we disagree on many things, I consider them my most valued friends.

I also thank several people at the Miami–Dade Medical Examiner's Office: Dr. James Davis, Dr. Ray Fernandez, Veronica Melton-Lamar, and Kayshone Wright. Professor William Wilbanks also left his homicide books and personal Miami homicide files for me after his retirement from Florida International University. I thank him for those records. I also thank others who helped me in Miami but whose names are temporarily misplaced.

The MPD connections led to others. A meeting on police brutality at the Police Foundation, and Steve Mastrofski's introduction, allowed me to meet former San Diego Police Department (SDPD) chief Jerry Sanders. Chief Sanders led me to 1401 Broadway, and Lt. Glenn Breitenstein and Lt. Jim Collins let me into the SDPD. I also thank James F. Hergenroeather and L. D. Martin, detectives in the SDPD homicide office. S. Fernando Rodriguez provided both El Paso homicide data and insight into the contours of the city. Howard Daudistel supported that effort. My thanks to both of them. Victoria Brewer Titterington graciously shared Houston homicide data. I thank her for that as well.

Initiation and completion of this book was enhanced greatly by the University of Delaware Department of Sociology and Criminal Justice and the College of Arts and Sciences. I am in great debt to my former deans, Mary Richards and Margaret Andersen, for generous support. They provided funds and a course reduction when other sources temporarily dried up at a crucial time and gave me the opportunity to pursue a project that required an enormous amount of time away from my office. I also thank my former departmental colleagues at UD who took up the slack during time away from my desk. I miss them all.

The National Science Foundation, a Ford Foundation Postdoctoral

Fellowship for Minorities, the Harry Frank Guggenheim Foundation, and the National Consortium on Violence Research provided funds to conduct this project, and I thank them for the assistance. NCOVR also provided a community of scholars who served as a source of information and inspiration. In fact, the idea of writing this book was started in Al Blumstein's backyard during an NCOVR picnic, and many members provided encouragement, criticisms, and comments from that moment until completion of the manuscript. Richard Rosenfeld suggested I write a book on Latino homicide; John Hagan thought the idea was worth pursuing; and Al and many others, including Pat Edgar and Darnell Hawkins, supported funding a grant that looked at Latino homicides in five cities, and the assistance proved crucial in developing this project. Robert Bursik and Ralph Taylor (twice) read and critiqued the entire manuscript while under their own sentences of journal editor and departmental chair, respectively. Diego Vigil, Eduardo Bonilla-Silva, Richard Rosenfeld, and Abel Valenzuela also provided comments on various parts of this book. Valenzuela's observations, especially, inform the crux of this book, chapters 4 and 5, and I thank him for critiquing while compiling his tenure dossier.

I owe a debt of gratitude to several former students who helped in reading, coding, and storing the homicide reports. Two deserve special thanks and recognition. Karen Jacobs started working on this project as a sophomore, and her energy and enthusiasm never waned, even while working long hours at poor pay. Matthew T. Lee joined this project close to its inception while completing his master's thesis and eventually turned parts of this effort into a dissertation; we continue research collaboration. It is impossible to adequately express my thanks to Matt for helping me dig through boxes in Miami; careful data management; incisive readings of the manuscript while doing his own work; and his encouragement to continue and complete this book, especially after several highly placed friends were ousted from the MPD after Elian's retrieval and I feared that data access had been terminated. Matt assured me that I was an "MPD insider" and data were still available, and he was right. My debt to him goes far beyond what I owe him as a colleague and a friend.

I would also like to point out that while support for affirmative action programs is under attack, it would have been difficult to make this contribution without the opportunities they permit and the individuals who administer them. I am proud to have received funding from the American Sociological Association and Ford Foundation minority fellowship programs. Ohio State University provided a graduate school minority fellowship, which wooed me away from my birthplace of San Antonio, Texas. I also thank the University of Delaware for hiring me on a target-of-opportunity line. Pundits criticize these programs, but I am still waiting for someone else to take seriously the study of Latinos and crime, both as fundamental to their professional identity and as a personal commitment. This book is evidence that these programs work.

Forums that helped focus this project, especially in the early writing stages, sharpened some of the ideas presented later in the book. I thank the Julian Samora Research Institute at Michigan State University, the Presley Center for Crime and Justice Studies at the University of California at Riverside, and the Center for the Study of Urban Poverty at the University of California at Los Angeles for inviting me to give talks and presentations. I want to express special gratitude to center directors Robert Nash Parker, Diego Vigil, Abel Valenzuela, and Refugio Rochin. While on leave or sabbatical, the Departments of Sociology at the University of Miami, the University of Michigan, and Bowling Green State University generously provided office space, and I thank them for it. The National Institute of Justice also provided a forum for speaking on the immigration and crime findings during a research conference plenary session in July 2000. Portions of "Immigration and Crime," in *National Institute of Justice Criminal Justice 2000: The Nature of Crime: Continuity and Change,* vol. 1, pp. 485–524, are used in chapters 2 and 3.

Mario Martinez, Sammi Nielsen, and Max Martinez-Nielsen provided constant support, warmth, and affection with little complaints. There were times they wanted to play and I didn't, but eventually I played anyway. Last, I'm indebted to Amie L. Nielsen for her unwavering love, understanding, and comments, which helped me in inestimable ways. My apologies to her for extended absences over the data collection, entry, and analysis period, which extended several years longer than I originally thought, and for my many foul moods when writing was going poorly or usually not at all. I hope this book was worth the loss of my companionship during critical times, but I missed you as much as you missed me.

LATINO HOMICIDE

1. INTRODUCTION
Latinos and Violent Crime

THE CURRENT CENTURY started much like the previous one—many people are debating the costs and consequences of letting newcomers into American society, and immigration remains a divisive topic.[1] One consequence of immigration is evident—the Latino population more than doubled between 1980 and 2000, from 14.5 million to an estimated 35.3 million, and now equals African Americans as the largest ethnic minority group.[2] The bulk of that growth resulted from the rise in the number of recent immigrants, who represent approximately a third of the total Latino population and 10 percent of all Americans.[3] Largely because of their visibility and size, the immigration debate focuses heavily on Latinos, and many problems associated with immigrants in the public imagination—loss of well-paying jobs, rise in urban decay, intergroup conflict,[4] and crime—are linked to Latinos.

Heightened immigration coincided with the upsurge in youth/ gang and drug-related homicide in the 1980s (and early 1990s), and these events deeply troubled many Americans to the extent that both issues are considered pressing national problems. For better or worse, concern over the roots of this urban crisis is partially directed at Latinos. Spurred to a large extent by alarm over violent crime, immigration opponents linked crime to foreign-born Latinos, and this presumed connection[5] was exacerbated by at least two dramatic events: the 1980 boatlift from Mariel, Cuba, which resulted in more than 125,000 Cubans landing in southern Florida; and the widely publicized movement throughout the 1980s and early 1990s of undocumented Mexicans crossing the border into the southwestern United States. Political pundits and

1

immigration opponents used these developments to highlight the failure of immigration policy and to heighten public concern that the U.S.–Mexican border was "out of control."[6] It was obvious, according to some, that many criminally inclined refugees were allowed to freely enter our country undeterred and did so with little fear of sanction.[7]

These fears are borne by documented and undocumented Latino residents, both noncitizens and citizens alike, as more Latinos arrived in the United States, undistinguishable from those who have been here for generations. Partly as a response to the recent Latino prominence and partly as an attempt to address stereotypes and combat the public unease with Latinos, scholarly interest in Latinos rose in many areas, such as history, political science, demography, public policy, immigration, and ethnic studies.[8] Perhaps the most important legacy of the rise of Latino research was that the national fixation with race now concentrated on an ethnic group comprised of both established and more recent Americans.[9] Surprisingly, research on Latino crime remained virtually untouched, even though media stereotypes on the Latino criminal date back to the turn of the last century, morphing from bandit to gang member over the years, and this image entered the public imagination and contemporary debate on the consequences of immigration.[10] Although Mariel Cubans are associated with drug-related violence, and Mexicans and Puerto Ricans with gang warfare in the popular media, relatively little is known about how much Latinos and Latino communities are influenced by violent crime such as homicide.

There are many unsubstantiated claims, contradictions, and assertions on this topic.[11] Given that widespread poverty is prevalent among persons of color, most writers assume that levels of Latino violence are similar to those of other ethnic minority groups[12] despite the existence of studies finding that Latino rates are comparable to Anglos or non-Latino Whites.[13] Still others predict rates between those of Whites and Blacks.[14] Widely shared assumptions about Latinos raise a series of fundamental yet unanswered questions: Aren't Latinos generally a crime-prone group? Isn't violence high on the Mexican border? Didn't the Mariel Cubans make Miami a violent city? Shouldn't the Latino homicide rate be higher than that of Anglos or as high as that of Blacks[15] in areas where Latinos dominate? Isn't violent crime the same for all Latino groups (Mexicans, Puerto Ricans, Central Americans, Cubans, etc.)? This volume is the first book-length attempt to answer these questions with hard evidence and empirical research that help us better understand the impact of the latest wave of Latino immigration.

Rather than narrowly focus on a specific Latino group, particular city, region of the country, or even specific year, my focus is on Latinos and Latino homicide in five cities[16]—Chicago, El Paso, Houston, Miami, and San Diego—that have faced extensive and sustained waves of immigration, and in the case of El Paso and San Diego, some of the longest history of Latino settlement in the United States.[17] The immigration process, in turn, should impact Latinos more than any other ethnic group and have a corresponding influence on homicide. But as we shall see, *the alleged immigration/crime link has had relatively little direct influence on Latinos. Latino homicide rates have not changed in a uniform manner. Instead, they have been characterized by exceptional variation across urban areas since 1980: some rose, others fell or even remained stable, but most remained lower than expected.*

The Latino population has experienced major social and demographic changes in the past twenty years—changes that are best captured at the city and neighborhood levels explored in this book.[18] Rapid population turnover and large numbers of immigrants have become distinguishing features of Latino communities—even those in El Paso and San Diego, where Latinos have existed for centuries. As foreign-born newcomers settled in areas with coethnics, fear of crime often increased.[19] However, homicides did not inundate all or even most Latino communities; many were concentrated in a small number of specific locations, while youth/drug-related killings in these areas did not always rise to unprecedented levels (as with other similarly situated ethnic minorities). By examining how Latino rates changed over time, with an emphasis on distinct types of homicide, as well as the correlates of these changes, I hope to provide insight into the relationships among Latinos; community conditions; and the serious, violent crime of homicide.

More specifically, my primary objectives are to describe and explain the extent of urban Latino homicide and to relate the patterns that emerge to other ethnic group patterns, to explore similarities and differences within the Latino population, and to determine the influences and circumstances that shape the nature of Latino homicides in urban communities. With the growth in numbers of Latinos—soon to be the largest ethnic minority group in the United States—writers and researchers have promoted a discussion about urban violence that rests on beliefs, guesses, and opinions about the latest threat to the national social fabric.[20] This book challenges the perceived nature of Latino criminality and the assumption that Latinos, especially young Latino males, are a criminally inclined ethnic group, by filling in the gaps in contemporary analyses of Latino violence.[21]

CURRENT CONTRIBUTIONS

Although it may be argued that there have been previous efforts in contemporary criminological research to study Latino homicide rates, it is not difficult to find evidence that Latinos have been overlooked in the violence literature.[22] As I will discuss extensively in chapter 3, most previous research reaches at least one conclusion similar to my findings: *The presence of Latino homicide is not as high as expected relative to that of other impoverished ethnic groups.* That conclusion may surprise some readers, in particular when one considers the moral panics cultivated by the media and police.[23] There are exceptions to this general rule, but nevertheless these are rare instances driven by specific and somewhat idiosyncratic circumstances. In spite of this consistent finding, important gaps remain to be studied that would undoubtedly contribute to a better understanding of Latino violence, illuminate broader issues common to other ethnic groups, and highlight some specific to Latinos. Therefore it is essential to more clearly highlight how the new insights about Latino homicides that have been generated in this book move beyond earlier research.

First, my approach builds on earlier studies in several ways. The analysis takes advantage of both individual-level and neighborhood-level homicide data.[24] Many people use one or the other, or in some instances examine national-level data.[25] These avenues are useful for some studies, but in my case combined sources reveal important differences across research settings, thereby suggesting a "kinds of place" rather than a "kinds of people" explanation of homicide. Not only do findings vary across and within cities, but also distinct variations in the effects of recent immigration have unfolded over time, especially 1980 through 1995, transforming the Latino population as well as patterns in Latino homicide.[26]

Equally important were the changing contemporary homicide contexts over the 1980s and 1990s, in particular pronounced levels of youth homicides, gang, and drug-related killings across urban America attributed largely to the crack cocaine epidemic.[27] If immigration changed the composition of the Latino population, heightened poverty, and increased crime, some writers[28] contend it should have done so during this time frame.[29] In fact, Latinos *should* have higher rates of homicide than other groups, or at least record high rates throughout the 1980s and 1990s.[30] More than a third of all Latinos are younger than eighteen years old (several years younger than Anglos and Blacks), many if not most are high school dropouts, and this high-risk age group is growing faster than any other segment of the American population.[31] All of the ingredients are present for an epidemic of Latino youth violence—their parents are poor, and these youth face a national backlash, are singled out for discrimination, compete for low-paying jobs with other ethnic minorities, and reside in impoverished areas often shaped by drugs and gangs, at least in the popular media's imagination. Yet the evidence is far from clear that a disproportionate number of Latinos, foreign or native-born, young or old, are enmeshed in violence.

Also important were the costs of punitive immigration policies in relation to Latinos and a burden not typically endured by other ethnic groups.[32] For instance, tougher immigration laws, relaxed deportation procedures, restrictive Immigration and Naturalization Service (INS) initiatives (e.g., Operation Hold the Line and Operation Gatekeeper), and more border police became routine and noticeable on the U.S.–Mexican border.[33] As a result, Latinos were simultaneously affected by a growth in human rights abuses among INS agents and local police, rising shooting deaths by law enforcement on the Mexican border, and a corresponding number of deaths as newcomers moved into isolated locales while crossing into the United States.[34] Finally, there is no doubt that since 1980 the arrival of millions of Latino immigrants fundamentally altered the demographic presence of an older Latino population in the United States[35] and changed the dynamics of Latino barrios or enclaves.[36] In addition to significantly enlarging the Latino population, this influx also to some extent reinforced the low economic position of Latinos. But the issue addressed in this book is whether this has engendered violent crime. My position is that it did not, at least to the extent that we might expect, given the dramatic changes and related underlying processes long associated with the effects of immigration on American cities.[37]

But these preliminary observations about Latinos and Latino homicide require additional explanation and background.[38] The central argument of this book is that *the most plausible explanation for Latino homicide patterns being lower than expected is the strength of Latino immigrants and immigrant communities, which buffer Latinos from criminal activity.* In fact, the more penetrating point is that Latinos have lower homicide rates than expected—be it at the national, city, or community level— because they exhibit higher levels of social integration, as measured by labor market involvement, while simultaneously exhibiting elevated poverty rates. Latinos, heavily immigrant, are poor but working, and that influence shapes homicide.[39]

LATINO EVIDENCE

In the Barrios: Latinos and the Underclass Debate (1993), a volume edited by Joan Moore and Raquel Pinderhughes, highlights the economic impact of Latino immigration in nine U.S. cities. In some areas, immigration has influenced the local economy by increasing marginal jobs for Latinos in the secondary sector, and has contributed to labor market competition with native-born Latinos as well as with other urban minority groups. Even though immigration is linked to heightened Latino poverty, many scholars describe a pool of Latino residents who are typically the "working poor" and attached to the labor market, although at times in the informal economy.[40]

In *The Truly Disadvantaged* (1987) and *When Work Disappears* (1996), William J. Wilson[41] describes how economic attachment is a key factor in maintaining family structures, stabilizing community institutions, and decreasing social problems in urban neighborhoods.[42] The anticipated consequence for crime and violence is that while Latino poverty rivals Black poverty, the impact on Latino violence is lower than expected because of greater attachment to the economy through low-paying but relatively steady jobs, along with lower rates of family disruption. This is a key interpretation investigated in chapter 3.

It is unclear whether the primary predictors of urban Latino criminal homicide are similar to those of other ethnic groups. Latino homicide rates are responsive to the same structural conditions as those of other groups, but those conditions differ across groups and within ethnic groups. For example, joblessness is not as widespread among most

Latino groups as among Blacks.[43] Latinos have high rates of labor force participation, but in lower-blue-collar occupations (operators, fabricators, and laborers) and in the informal economy (street vendors, domestics), fortifying my contention that Latinos are better characterized as the working poor than the chronically unemployed.[44] Also, nationwide, Latinos have a higher percentage of female-headed households than Anglos (21.6 percent vs. 11.8 percent) but substantially lower than Blacks (43.2 percent), based on national census data. Within the Latino population, Cubans have the lowest percent of female-headed households (16.3 percent), followed closely by Mexicans (18.2 percent). The Puerto Rican group has the highest proportion (36.6 percent), rivaling that of Blacks.[45] Thus traditional risk indicators for Anglo and Black homicide may need reevaluation and refinement for Latinos.

Nevertheless, some considerable contrasts in the economic and social circumstances of Blacks and Latinos can be observed in the five cities selected for this study. In table 1.1, however, I concentrate on Black and Latino comparisons, since, as seen more vividly in the next chapter, at the city level both groups are similarly situated (Latino ethnicity aside) in terms of economic deprivation, and non-Latino White data are not readily available. The levels of unemployment, male joblessness (which includes males not in the labor force), poverty, and female-headed households for Blacks and Latinos within and across the five cities are seen in table 1.1. One general observation is that absolute poverty characterizes the Latino population; at least a quarter of Latinos are impoverished in each of the cities. Latino poverty surpasses or rivals that of Blacks in the three southwestern cities.

Although the unemployment rate for Blacks and Latinos is similar across all these cities, strong group differences exist with respect to male joblessness and the percent of families headed by a female. In all cases, Black rates of male joblessness and female heads of families exceed those of Latinos. Further, the magnitude of these group differences varies across the cities. For example, rates of Black male joblessness and female-headed families are higher than the corresponding rates for Latinos in El Paso and San Diego; however, the differences between the two groups are relatively small. By comparison, in Houston and Chicago, Latino joblessness and Latina-headed families are *half* the levels of their Black counterparts. This contrast is stark considering that

TABLE 1.1

EMPLOYMENT, POVERTY, AND FAMILY STRUCTURE AMONG BLACKS
AND LATINOS IN FIVE MAJOR CITIES (PERCENTS)

	El Paso	San Diego	Houston	Chicago	Miami
Black					
Unemployed	8.4	7.6	9.8	11.4	10.7
Male joblessness	34.6	26.8	36.5	47.3	34.7
Poverty	15.9	23.1	30.6	33.2	46.0
Female-headed family	27.4	38.0	43.3	51.6	49.4
Latino					
Unemployed	7.3	6.4	6.4	8.2	6.0
Male joblessness	27.2	21.8	16.0	17.0	27.9
Poverty	32.5	25.6	30.7	24.2	28.5
Female-headed family	24.3	24.8	16.4	20.8	22.7

Source: U.S. Bureau of the Census, 1990.

African Americans have resided in Houston and Chicago for at least three or four generations, as have some Mexicans and to a lesser extent Puerto Ricans, but only recently have the numbers of Latinos risen to a large and identifiable mass.[46]

Miami provides yet another contrast. The difference between Black and Latino male joblessness is similar to El Paso and San Diego (about an 8 percent difference) but the large gap between Black-female- and Latina-headed families more closely resembles Houston and Chicago. In sum, while economic conditions vary for Blacks and Latinos—both groups tend to reside in highly impoverished areas—levels of traditional family structure and labor market participation are typically higher for Latinos. The differences across the cities in the ethnic contrasts present an important opportunity to explore the impact of social and economic circumstances on Latino homicides.

DATA ISSUES

Because of the study population's ethnic characteristics, the questions I posed required primary data collection. First, I collected almost three thousand homicide supplemental files from the city of Miami Police Department Homicide Investigations Unit in roughly the early to mid-

1990s period. These files included information on victim and suspect demographic characteristics (e.g., age, sex, race/ethnicity), a coding of the homicide motivation (e.g., drug, gang, robbery, etc.) based on a close reading of the detectives' account, previous victim and offender relationship, the crime scene address, and other information (e.g., weapon, alcohol use) that were coded into a questionnaire. This information generated data that were used to depict the circumstances surrounding homicide and victim/offender characteristics. I replicated the Miami gathering experiences in San Diego and El Paso (with assistance from S. Fernando Rodriguez) in 1996 and 1997, and accessed Houston data through Dr. Victoria Brewer as part of a multicity youth violence project developed in part for the National Consortium on Violence Research. The Chicago homicide data are a public dataset,[47] and the combined efforts of the other cities in this project were based on many of the coding schemes used in that source.

By using official internal police data I admittedly rely on the investigators' attention to detail, their perception of the killing based on witness, offender, and in some instances victim interviews, and, of course, consistency in the measurement of homicide.[48] Many observers criticize the use of police data given the potential of bias in reporting officially defined crimes, yet homicide is our most serious crime.[49] It is a very difficult crime to conceal, and it is much more reliably measured than other crimes.[50] Indeed, relevant to the purposes of this study, one of several strengths of a homicide report over a nonhomicide arrest report is the attention to detail on incidents, including ethnic characteristics, not readily available in other crimes. This does not necessarily mean that the findings in later chapters reflect other, less serious types of violence (e.g., armed robbery, aggravated assault), and they also might be different for property offenses. Yet few sources, cross-sectional or longitudinal, exist on Latinos and nonlethal assault and property crime that match these homicide data in consistency, detail, and accuracy.

A few more related points on data issues. To the extent possible, I direct attention to homicide offender rates (as in chapter 5) in the over-time analysis. The neighborhood investigation in chapters 3 and 4 measures the *presence* of homicide in a given community. To calculate tract-level homicide incidents as accurately as possible, and to count them to reflect neighborhood boundaries, I base homicide levels on where the victim is killed, for several reasons. First, information on the offender or suspect is missing or possibly unreliable in the substantial number of cases (about 25 percent in these cities) not cleared with an arrest. In addition, criminologist James F. Short points out that findings based on victimization data also are valid for offenders, given the intra-racial nature of the vast majority of homicide events.[51] Third, as in the case in chapter 6, many killings were victim-precipitated and the event turned lethal in large part due to circumstances initiated by the victim.

Furthermore, the motivations surrounding those killings, regardless of initiation, would not significantly differ if measured as offender moti-vation or victim precipitation. A robbery homicide indicates that the offender was motivated to rob and kill the victim. The end result is the same. Finally, the effects of structural conditions such as poverty on homicide victim and offending rates are substantially similar and pro-vide the same conclusions.[52] The closeness of this relationship is appar-ent in victim and offender graphs that followed very similar ebbs and flows over the 1980 through 1995 period (but that are not shown in the later chapters). Most victims and offenders reside in the same neighborhood, share similar surroundings, and are subject to almost identical pressures of everyday life.

THE ORGANIZATION OF THIS BOOK

Although the findings and conclusions presented in *Latino Homicide* are specific to the five cities in this book, many of my findings are perti-nent to Latino and Latina life across America and even life in America more generally. Because a majority of both native and foreign-born Latinos and Latinas live in cities much like El Paso, Chicago, Houston, San Diego, and Miami, my analysis is especially relevant to cities with long traditions of Latino entry and established Latino communities. Virtually every sizable city now has significant Latino populations, and Latinos encounter many routine problems beyond crime, such as lack of access to social justice and barriers to citizenship. The struggle to overcome exposure to crime, even hate crime, in American society re-quires similar responses to prejudices, stereotypes, subsistence pay, dan-gerous work conditions, profiling by official agencies, and hurdles to legality even after long periods of residency. In short, as a result of being singled out as crime-prone and dangerous predators, among other stereo-types, Latinos are responding to issues facing them in everyday life and forcing others to address their concerns. Latino clout is growing, and local, state, and national leaders should acknowledge and address the needs of this group.

In the larger context my book matters particularly in terms of racial/ethnic relations. My work does have larger implications, specifically recognizing that scapegoating ethnic minorities for a host of personal shortcomings or social problems, perpetuating negative portrayals and blaming others, damages more than it repairs American society. Fears and concerns over an increasingly multiethnic country obscure the fact that there is little danger of replacing one ethnic group with another, an alarm raised by many immigration opponents, and the realization that many U.S. residents have long lived in diverse communities. Instead, rather than attacking any specific ethnic group, inclusion and full participation are necessary to accommodate those previously excluded, intentionally or not. All issues considered, it is probable that just treatment will in the long run reduce crime, while insisting that some groups are a threat to the social fabric of society will perpetuate it. The latter creates more resentment and breeds more frustration, factors that have long been at the core of sociological explanations of crime.[53]

Throughout this book I attempt to draw an expansive picture that connects the past to the present and cuts across several academic disciplines while still making the entire process a coherent focus on Latinos and Latino violence.[54] I begin chapter 2 by exploring theoretical approaches and past research on immigration, Latinos, and crime. While these perspectives are not directly tested, they do provide the rationale for examining Latinos as a distinct and separate group, as well as framing the discussion of the findings. Early and recent immigrant crime studies, some of which examine Latinos, are reviewed to further establish the specific ways in which Latinos are both similar to and different from other U.S. ethnic minority groups. Moreover, I furnish more detail on how the Chicago School established an urban research baseline that later seemed to emphasize a Black/White dichotomy.

Chapter 3 extends the foundation for this study in terms of research settings, identity, time frame, and, of course, the immigration/homicide nexus, and then proceeds to consider what the best (but limited) available national information reveals relating to these considerations. When appropriate, Latinos are compared to other ethnic groups. In chapter 4 I elaborate on the formation of Latino communities and provide a view of the twenty barrios and enclaves explored in this book. To provide further comparisons on racial/ethnic variations, I contrast the presence of Whites/Blacks and others to Latinos and show the intra-Latino variations in the five cities, with Puerto Ricans, Central Americans, and Cubans joining the primarily Mexican populations.

Armed with a clear picture of Latino communities, chapter 5 provides cross-city and cross-community comparisons of urban Latino homicides. Supplied with an array of information on Latinos and Latino homicide, I focus on communities in all five cities and provide comparisons to similarly sized cities. Next, I explore the level of several homicide motives, showing that while economic conditions in Latino communities are typically substandard, the gang/drug epidemic did not hit these barrios and enclaves as hard as the rest of urban America.

In chapter 6 I focus on Latino homicide levels relative to Anglos and Blacks over the 1980 to 1995 time period. I also extend and elaborate on these ethnic group comparisons by examining the role of gender and age. Contrary to widespread notions, Latino males are not as heavily involved in violence as popularly portrayed. Chapter 7 focuses on various types of homicide motivation (e.g., intimate, drug, gang, robbery, escalation, and other felony) to explore the full array of lethal violence. Some are unexpectedly rare but as expected most are mundane arguments turned lethal. Having described the Latino homicide experience, I turn to two special cases that served to inflame the public's "moral panic" toward the subject of violence among Latinos—the Mariels in Miami and Mexican-origin border crossers in San Diego—with special emphasis on the individual and spatial factors influencing homicide.

Finally, a concluding chapter presents suggestions on future research on ethnic differences in homicide patterns. Based on the work of other researchers and the findings presented here, this concluding chapter makes clear how much more research remains on the subject of Latino violence. Still, this is the first book-length manuscript on the subject of Latino violence and homicides, and it corrects the longstanding image of crime-prone Latinos. Contrary to stereotypes and counter to what we would expect based on residence in extremely poor communities, not only are Latinos not typically crime driven, they are not typically homicidal.

2. THE LEGACY AND IMAGES OF LATINO CRIME

THE MOST PREVALENT IMAGE of Mexicans in popular culture is, of course, the violent bandit or "bandito"—an image fixed in the early 1900s by makers of silent films but popularized since then by a host of writers, television executives, and the contemporary motion picture industry.[1] The immigrant criminal has always projected a violent image in the public imagination, but the creation of a "Latino bandito" formed a new caricature and gave life to a new ethnic stereotype. The Mexican bandit was often portrayed as excessively violent in films of the American West such as *The Cowboys' Baby* (1910), *Tony the Greaser* (1911), and several others.[2] The violent bandit robbed, killed, pillaged, and plundered onscreen, killing children and raping women in a series of cowboy-Western films between 1910 and 1916.[3]

This stereotype to a certain extent flourished on film because of sensationalistic journalist coverage of a nonfiction event: the Mexican Revolution of 1910. Newspapers documented the actions of Mexican revolutionaries on the battlefield, depicting bloodshed on the field between troops, translating real images of violence into fictional images of banditry, and in turn transforming the bandito into a criminal bent on violence. The stereotype of a bloodthirsty Mexican bandit became embedded in the public imagination. Mexicans were violent on the battlefield and off of it.

The violent immigrant or violence-prone Latino, however, is a social construct with a distinct history in the social sciences.[4] The Mexi-

13

can Revolution created massive upheaval and led to an exodus of thousands of people to the United States. Yet most Americans at the time were more concerned about the appearance of European immigrants in the Midwest and along the eastern seaboard. For example, immigration restriction advocates in the early 1900s contended that immigrant groups were "biologically deficient compared with nonimmigrants" and that "crime was one of many harmful products that could be expected as long as 'inferior' immigrants were allowed to enter the country." In a 1939 special report[5] to a New York State commission, Harry Laughlin wrote in "Immigration and Conquest" that immigration was "likely to destroy the inherent racial and family-stock qualities—physical, mental, and spiritual—of the people of the immigrant-receiving country." This body of biologically inclined writing was associated with the long since disgraced eugenics movement, and although it failed to provide solid empirical evidence to back such claims, these ideas did guide U.S. immigration legislation in the 1920s, which severely limited immigration from non-European countries.[6]

This chapter will draw on several theoretical elements and schools of thought that have guided explanations of the immigration-crime link. While early stereotypes drive the conventional wisdom on the relationship between Latinos and homicide—the violent bandit gradually morphed into the gang member and criminal alien—other aspects of the immigration and crime link had previously experienced substantial intellectual development. The massive wave of European immigrants to the United States in the early 1900s prompted social scientists to concentrate on various aspects of the consequences of immigration. Much like now, many people feared the presence of newcomers entering American society.[7] This concern encouraged a closer look at the nature of urban crime and criminals. In fact, contemporary research is grounded in past and sometimes overlooked work that is still relevant to the situations of old and new Latinos in contemporary society.

THEORETICAL APPROACHES

A variety of approaches have been proposed to make sense of the voluminous and often contradictory data produced by research on the relationship between immigration and crime.[8] Some current theories tend to emphasize stress related to acculturation pressures, or more often, sociological variables (e.g., community disorganization) as a rationale for why immigrants should be affected by crime more than others, or why immigrant communities should have high crime rates. There is some disagreement as to the relative importance of different factors, but most theoretical work can be classified into one of the major perspectives mentioned in the next section—perspectives that grew out of a century of scholarly interest in crime and criminal behavior.

Opportunity Structure

Scholars have consistently noted the tendency for new immigrants to settle in urban neighborhoods characterized by poverty, substandard housing, poor schools, and high crime rates.[9] Segregated in such neighborhoods, immigrants may turn to crime as a means to overcome blocked economic opportunities. Other writers have suggested that previously noncriminal immigrant groups may simply be "contaminated" by the criminal opportunities that abound in their neighborhoods.[10] According to this view, immigrant criminality is more a function of preexisting structural factors such as poverty,[11] a preponderance of young, unattached males,[12] or the availability of alcohol,[13] than either the biological makeup or cultural traditions of immigrant groups.

Much of the early criminological research on immigrants focused on youth groups and the importance of group conflict in creating gangs.[14] In the first careful study of gangs, Frederic Thrasher described in his book *The Gang* how youth groups initially were spontaneously formed but eventually solidified in the face of escalating arguments with other juveniles.[15] The pressure to resist outside threats, in this and other cases, helped define gang identity and increased gang formation, as well as leading to serious crime across the life course of gang members.[16]

Shortly after the publication of Thrasher's seminal piece in 1927, existing stereotypes of Latino (Mexican-origin) youth as a "bandito" began to shift to the image of a criminally inclined, vicious, and treacherous zoot-suit-wearing gang member.[17] This reflection mirrored the World War II–era national hysteria over juvenile crime and contributed to heightened attention to this new ethnic group. The popular press and public officials began to argue that levels of Mexican juvenile delinquency were growing and could potentially present a threat to the stability of Los Angeles society.[18] In a report to a special grand jury committee appointed to investigate this issue, Capt. E. Duran Ayres of the Los Angeles Sheriff's Office Foreign Relations Bureau[19] noted that the potential explanations of Mexican delinquency were rooted in local conditions: "Discrimination and segregation, as evidenced by public signs and rules, such as appear in certain restaurants, public swimming plunges, public parks, theaters, and even in schools, cause resentment among the Mexican people. . . . All this applies to both the foreign and American-born Mexicans."

While acknowledging the discriminatory practices of the Greater Los Angeles society, Ayres continues to note in his conclusions that ". . . the Anglo-Saxon, when engaged in fighting, particularly among youths, resort to fisticuffs and may at times kick each other, which is considered unsportive: but this Mexican element considers all that to be a sign of weakness, and all he knows and feels is a desire to use a knife or some lethal weapon. In other words, his desire is to kill, or at least let blood. . . . When there is added to this inborn characteristic that had come down through the ages, the use of liquor, then we certainly have crimes of violence." This official document symbolized the official view that "Mexicans possessed an inborn tendency to criminal behavior and to crimes of violence."[20] The linkage of race and criminality thrust Mexican youths into the public consciousness, partially replacing the bandit image with that of a dangerous urban gang member. While this attention highlighted Latinos, it also fueled existing hostility from social institutions such as the police, schools, and local governments that did not subside until the early 1960s.[21]

These examples of the way people viewed Latinos are important because contemporary immigrant gangs can be viewed as alternative means of securing wealth and status in urban areas where immigrants are concentrated, where a loss of blue-collar jobs has eroded the principal basis of upward mobility used by earlier generations of immigrants.[22] Patterns of factory life associated with the industrial revolution socialized earlier waves of immigrants (e.g., Irish and Italians) and facilitated their economic stability and assimilation into American culture, thus suppressing their crime rates.[23] But the recent loss of industrial jobs, traceable to the late-twentieth-century transition of the economy from a manufacturing to a service orientation, has had drastic consequences on legitimate (and illegitimate) opportunities in American cities.[24] Although this economic effect impacts both immigrants and nonimmigrants, newcomers (who are both economically and culturally marginal in American society) may find the potential benefits of the underground economy particularly attractive.[25] Since the possibility of gang membership is limited, and is in fact usually based on ethnic identity, among other factors,[26] the availability of illegitimate opportunities in gangs is one structural variable that differentially influences immigrant crime across social units such as cities or neighborhoods.

CULTURAL APPROACHES

In addition to this list of structural issues, scholars have viewed cultural forces as influencing criminal involvement, and immigrant crime in particular. The "culture of poverty" thesis—where low-income people adapt to their structural conditions in ways that tend to perpetuate their disadvantaged condition—is one example of a cultural explanation of criminal activity.[27] Thus engaging in crime as a means of acquiring social status draws children away from schoolwork, which reduces the probability of future economic advancement, since a lack of education hinders job prospects. A variant of this explanation for crime, the "subculture of violence" thesis, suggests that violence can become a "normal" and expected means of dispute resolution in disadvantaged areas.[28] For example, homicides that occur among lower-class people frequently grew out of minor slights that took on substantial significance because of commonly held expectations about how people would act in routine situations.[29] Marvin Wolfgang provides the following illustration in *Patterns in Criminal Homicide:* "A male is usually expected to defend the name or honor of his mother, the virtue of womanhood . . . and to accept no derogation about his race, his age, or his masculinity. Quick resort to physical combat as a measure of daring, courage, or defense of status appears to be a cultural expression, especially for lower socioeconomic class males of 'both' races. When such a culture norm response is elicited from an individual engaged in social interplay with others who harbor the same response mechanism, physical assaults, altercations, and violent domestic quarrels that result in homicide are likely to be common."

Because immigrants and ethnic minorities are more likely than native-born Whites to reside in lower-income areas, these cultural theories seem particularly useful. Of course, as Sampson and Lauritsen[30] point out, the subculture-of-violence theory cannot explain the wide variations in violent crime rates across structurally diverse ethnic minority neighborhoods, and they conclude that structural conditions are ultimately more important than cultural traditions.

Nevertheless, some writers argue that certain types of crime are more prevalent among specific immigrant groups because of cultural traditions brought from the home country. Both Edwin Sutherland[31] and Thorsten Sellin[32] argued that immigrant groups had "cultural predispositions" toward certain crimes. For example, in the 1920s Italians had high rates of conviction for homicide but low rates of arrests for drunkenness.[33] A study of Hawaii during the same period revealed that Chinese immigrants brought with them traditions of certain types of graft and gambling.[34]

Another body of literature in the cultural tradition has focused on the processes by which immigrants adapt to the traditions of the host country.[35] It has long been asserted that acculturation to a new environment involves "adjustment to heterogeneous conduct norms" and that this, in turn, can lead to higher crime rates.[36] Thorsten Sellin provides a classic example in *Culture Conflict and Crime*: "A few years ago a Sicilian father in New Jersey killed the sixteen-year-old seducer of his daughter, expressing surprise at his arrest since he had merely defended his family honor in a traditional way." In contrast, immigrant gangs, for example, usually owe as much to American cultural tradition as those of the immigrant culture, to the point where adult Vietnamese refer to Vietnamese delinquents as "Americanized."[37] Immigrant gangs also form as a reaction to ethnic tensions in diverse neighborhoods; they provide physical protection from other ethnic-based gangs and maintain ethnic identities in the face of pressures for assimilation.[38]

Those cases again underscore the importance of generational status and crime rates. Historical works on European immigrants and locally raised first-generation children lead us to expect an increase in violence. Immigrants and their children are widely believed to engage in crime at higher levels than native-born people because of cultural adjustments, including exposure to higher levels of crime. In other words, as urban immigrants become "Americanized" and socialized into violent postures by inner-city neighbors, crime should rise among this group and within the communities where immigrant children reside.[39]

SOCIAL DISORGANIZATION

The social disorganization perspective adds to the other perspectives a concern with the breakdown of community social institutions that result from social change. Robert Bursik[40] describes disorganized areas as possessing an "inability to realize the common values of their residents or solve commonly expressed problems." In organized neighborhoods, local community institutions work together to realize community goals, protect values, and generally control the behavior of community members in ways that conform to these goals and values. Bankston[41] notes that immigration may undermine established institutions via a process of population turnover, while it also makes agreement about common values more difficult. The implication is that when social control is weakened in this manner, crime will flourish.

W. I. Thomas and Florian Znaniecki[42] set forth one early influential statement of this perspective in their five-volume work published between 1918 and 1920 titled *The Polish Peasant in Europe and America.* Thomas and Znaniecki wrote about the many social changes affecting Polish peasants in this period, including the disorganizing influences inherent in moving from simple, homogeneous, rural areas of Poland to complex, heterogeneous, urban areas in the United States. They defined social disorganization as "a decrease of the influence of existing social rules of behavior upon individual members of the group."[43] The effectiveness of social rules (e.g., laws) derived from the individual's investment in them (e.g., attitudes favorable to laws). In the organized society, there was congruence between group rules and individual attitudes. Disorganization implied a gap between rules and attitudes, such that an individual did not feel bound by the rules and was free to disobey them (e.g., engage in crime). Viewed in this light, disorganization was a neutral term that suggested the possibility of social change, both positive and negative, and individual liberation from oppressive community standards, although it has generally been applied to studies of crime. One contribution of this literature is the recognition that crime is not only a function of structural (e.g., poverty) or cultural (e.g., "subculture of violence") forces but also is intimately tied to the fundamental processes of social change.

Although not chiefly concerned with crime, Thomas and Znaniecki[44] did apply the idea of disorganization to the crimes of Polish immigrants. Murder among the Polish, for example, had a very different etiology in Poland as compared to the United States. Murder among the Polish in Poland was predominantly confined to one's own small communal group—murders of strangers were rare. The motive (e.g., revenge) in these cases was most often strongly felt and was preceded by long periods of brooding and a sense of violating deeply held values. In contrast, murder in America by Polish immigrants was more likely to involve a victim who was a stranger or not well known to the offender, and less likely to involve concern with the seriousness of violating standards of the community. In the disorganized areas of America into which Polish immigrants settled, the social ties of the old country were weakened and community controls were loosened. Freed from traditional social controls and subjected to social forces that affected their lives in ways they could not control or sometimes understand, some Polish immigrants exhibited "general nervousness" and "vague expectation of hostility" that were virtually unknown in the old country.[45] In such circumstances, murder could be provoked by seemingly trivial offenses partly because the immigrant feels the need to take individual action against affronts. Since the weakened Polish community in America was not able to solve disputes and organize behavior as it had in the old country, a host of social problems increased, including crime.

Despite the voluminous work of Thomas and Znaniecki, scholars most often associate the social disorganization perspective with the writings of Shaw and McKay in *Juvenile Delinquency and Urban Areas* on the ecological distribution of delinquency.[46] Shaw and McKay utilized the concept of social disorganization to great effect by using quantitative data from Chicago neighborhoods to specify the role of community disorganization in producing high crime rates, other conditions (e.g., poverty and ethnicity) being equal. Their most important finding was that "within the same type of social area, the foreign-born and the natives, recent immigrant nationalities, and older immigrants produce very similar rates of delinquents."[47] Or in the words of one of their critics, "nativity and nationality have no vital relationship to juvenile delinquency."[48] The Chicago data suggested to Shaw and McKay that certain areas had consistently high rates of delinquency, regardless of which immigrant groups lived there, and that as immigrant groups moved out of these areas and into better neighborhoods their juvenile delinquency rates fell as well.

Inspired by Thomas and Znaniecki, the theoretical explanation suggested by these patterns was that neighborhoods characterized by "disorganizing" factors such as high population turnover and ethnic heterogeneity will be less likely than other neighborhoods to control the behavior of their inhabitants. According to this view, immigrants will have high crime rates only when they settle in disorganized neighborhoods, not because of biological factors or criminal cultural traditions. Thus, as an example, theory and research suggest that crime should flourish in areas characterized by economic deprivation and other deleterious social conditions because residents exert little control over disorganized communities.

Recent theoretical work by Sampson and Lauritsen[49] has attempted to demonstrate how macrosocial and local community-level structural forces can be combined to improve on the classic disorganization framework. Although this work developed from an attempt to explain Black/White crime differences, as well as the wide variation in Black crime rates across structurally different community areas, they also advance our knowledge of the link between immigration/ethnicity and crime. Powerful generic social processes (e.g., segregation, housing discrimination, and structural transformation of the economy) coincide with local community-level factors (e.g., residential turnover, concentrated poverty, and family disruption) to impede the social organization of inner cities.[50] A deeper understanding of the complex effects of these variables would enhance existing theories by better incorporating the role of the "massive social change" experienced by the mostly black residents in U.S. inner cities in the 1970s and 1980s.[51] Since the latest immigration wave brought newcomers into these same structural conditions,[52] and some argue that they accelerated these conditions,[53] we might expect high rates of immigrant crime during this (and the earlier) time period.[54] This question is the subject of the next sections on Latinos and crime.

EMPIRICAL STUDIES

Early Empirical Studies

In a recent historical study of homicide in the United States, Roger Lane, in *Murder in America: A History,*[55] concludes that "homicide in the modern world has been mostly an irrationally impulsive crime, com-

mitted by young men, especially poor and aimless young men ener-
gized by frustration and anger." This book sets the story of homicide
within the wider history of America and across an array of social or historical conditions, including the movement into cities from abroad.
Since immigrants, at least initially, tend to include a disproportionate
number of young males, it might be expected that they exhibit higher
crime rates than the native population. This has been the case in some
instances during a specific time period.[56] Beyond this population issue,
the three theoretical perspectives previously discussed offer compelling
reasons for why immigrants should have high crime rates: they usually
settle in high-poverty, high-crime, disorganized communities and encounter problems of adjustment that native groups do not experience.
Also, many immigrants move from rural areas into center cities, and this
also exerts a disorganizing influence on communal and familial structures.[57] In fact, urban growth and immigration usually occur simultaneously, and increases in crime are often more a function of urbanization
than any other factor.[58] To highlight, *the major finding of a century of
research on immigration and crime is that while immigrants occasionally
displayed tremendous variations across time and place in their criminal
involvement, contrary to popular opinion they nearly always exhibit lower
crime rates than native groups.*[59]

The earliest studies on crime among the first wave of heavily European immigrants, which ended in 1924, were based on crime data that
were uneven at best.[60] These studies suggested that newcomers were
less likely to be involved in crime than the native-born. A special report
issued by the Industrial Commission of 1901 found that "foreign-born
whites were less criminal than native whites," while the 1911 Immigration Commission concluded, "immigration has not increased the volume of crime" and that the presence of immigrants may have even
suppressed criminal activity.[61] A review of other early immigrant/crime
studies showed that contrary to stereotypes, most researchers did not
find the first-wave immigrants to be highly crime-prone,[62] although
results did vary by city.[63] These studies generally found that children of
immigrants had higher crime rates than their immigrant parents, but
not always higher than native-born children. This suggests that the
acculturation to American life of the second generation of immigrants,
and not the assumed "criminal traditions" of immigrant groups, was

related to immigrant crime rates.[64] But again, even if acculturation weakened the impact of traditional social controls in some immigrant communities, these early reports found that immigrants generally remained less crime-prone than natives.

A prominent report published in 1931 by the National Commission on Law Observance and Enforcement, popularly known as the Wickersham Report, noted that immigrants had lower overall crime rates than nonimmigrants, although some groups appeared disproportionately involved in specific types of crime. Mexicans in one study, for example, displayed higher rates of arrest for some violent crimes than native Whites.[65] However, in another study published in that report, Paul S. Taylor was able to draw several conclusions. First, Mexican crime rates seemed to be in line or proportionate with population size. Second, patterns of criminal involvement varied considerably across cities and were shaped by a host of social factors, including poverty and the age and sex distributions of the immigrant population. Paul S. Taylor[66] also discovered that Mexican criminal involvement displayed "interesting diversity within the same locality," suggesting the need to examine structural factors differentially affecting immigrants in socially meaningful areas such as neighborhoods, rather than larger entities such as cities and states.

Moreover, the Wickersham Report was published during a time when many citizens assumed the inherent criminality of Latino youths and young adults.[67] For example, Taylor[68] found policemen who thought Mexicans were fierce and prone to dangerous and disorderly behavior. Other report contributors echoed comments regarding Mexican criminality, explaining that they were "*malos hombres* that carried a knife or gun around," were vocal in the streets and at home, frequently fighting and assaulting friends and acquaintances, according to interviews with public officials. Despite these popular stereotypes, the Wickersham Report was instrumental in at least one way—it portrayed Latino violence in areas with a large and visible Latino population as a relatively rare event. In short, pioneering homicide studies largely contrasted and compared European immigrants to African Americans in Chicago, Philadelphia, and New York City,[69] but few scholars acknowledged the presence of Latinos in the southwestern United States and other parts of the country, so Latino research largely disappeared after the publication of this report, and crime research focused on Black and White comparisons.[70]

Contemporary Empirical Studies

Although a host of reasons exist to expect that immigrants are high-crime-prone and despite the media portrayal of Mexicans as violent bandits, the bulk of empirical studies conducted over the past century have found that immigrants in general and Mexicans in particular are typically not overrepresented in criminal statistics. As we will see in the following section, this finding usually holds across time and varying community contexts. This is important because it serves as a reminder that some ethnic minority groups such as Latinos, compared to native-born groups, are able to withstand deleterious conditions conducive to crime and others are not. A fuller appreciation of this literature is necessary to understand the immigrant-crime relationship and to make sense of its impact on urban American society.

What follows is a chronicle of Latino homicide research; it is an exhaustive but concise account that highlights the links between local conditions and ethnic comparisons, and initially concentrates on Mexicans in the Southwest, who constitute the majority of this country's Latino population and primary source of immigrants. This section also updates the Wickersham Report by exploring the extent of Latino homicide offending in contemporary America.

Scholarly research and public concern about immigration and crime practically disappeared in the middle third of the twentieth century.[71] This is not surprising, since immigration was low during this period, and large segments of the first wave had been assimilated into American society.[72] But the recent wave of immigration (largely Latino, Asian, and Afro Caribbean) has generated renewed interest in the topic, in part because the arrival of these immigrants coincided with the rise in crime rates in this country during the late 1960s and 1970s.

Recent studies of the nongang criminal involvement of specific immigrant or ethnic groups have been rare.[73] The studies that have been conducted tend to agree with research on the first wave: the incidence and prevalence of immigrant Latino crime is often much lower than for native-born ethnic groups. For example, research on homicide in San Antonio found that homicide rates among Mexican males over the 1940 through 1980 period fell between those of native Whites and Blacks, and that homicide remained concentrated in downtown areas of the city, regardless of whether the residents were Black or Mexican.[74] This is important to highlight, since Mexicans fleeing strife in their home country between 1890 and 1930 greatly enlarged existing barrios in the southwestern United States. But there was no evidence of a corresponding increase of homicide, at least in San Antonio.

In 1955 some homicide researchers began to focus their attention directly on Latinos.[75] Examining Houston, Texas, murders from 1945 through 1949, Bullock discovered that, similar to the classic work of Shaw and McKay in Chicago, Latinos (Mexicans) were residing in high-crime areas adjacent to the central business district. Thus Latinos displayed a settlement pattern resembling that of earlier European immigrants, again highlighting the linkage between neighborhood conditions and crime, but for the first time this ecological connection for Latinos was documented in a large Sunbelt city.

Several other homicide studies in Houston extended the new focus on Latinos. Alex D. Pokorny[76] provided an analysis of Anglo, Black, and Latino lethal violence, using 1960 crime data, and discovered that Latino homicide victim and offender rates fell between those of Whites and Blacks—Latino rates were twice those of Anglos but a third less than those of Blacks. Pokorny's work thus served as an early indicator that important differences distinguished Latinos from other ethnic groups, thus warranting further study.

Two other Houston studies[77] that appeared in scholarly journals by Beasley and Antunes and by Mladenka and Hill incorporated "percent Mexican American" as a predictor of index crime (including homicide) in Houston police districts. While not directly estimating the extent and severity of Latino homicide, two important points emerged from these studies. First, these scholars continued to concentrate on the importance of the Mexican subjects in a major urban city.[78] Second, while findings from both studies were limited because of high correlations with population density and low income (and other factors) in Houston, they again highlight the considerable role of local conditions in homicide research—a direction followed in the remainder of this book.

Shifting the focus north, Chicago provided another foundation for studying the immigration/crime link. Even though the Windy City has an old and visible Mexican and Puerto Rican population,[79] only a handful of studies on Latino homicide in this city exist in the literature. Becky Block[80] noted the contributions of Latinos to the overall patterns of Chicago homicides from 1965 to 1981. She found that the

Latino homicide rate had increased at a much faster rate than the Latino population size. In contrast, Anglo and Black homicide rates resembled respective group growth (or decline) over the time period in this study. Block offers a plausible explanation for this difference: the Latino influx overburdened Latino community structures, making them unable to assist the newcomers, lessening local control, and in turn increasing homicide. Block (1993) later reported that young Latino males were at a far greater risk than any other Latino gender or age group. In fact, the homicide rate for Latino males fifteen to twenty-nine years of age matched that of their Black counterparts. With that exception, however, most Latino homicide victim rates fell between Anglo and Black rates.

A more recent study found that immigration was not related to youth violence in California, while alcohol availability was an important influence on serious crime among young males in three cities with a heavy Latino population.[81] In fact, the high number of alcohol outlets was one of the leading contributors to crime. Finally, a study of Puerto Rican newcomers found that those living in New York City had high rates of homicide, while Puerto Ricans living elsewhere had rates comparable to those of native Whites.[82]

Research by Wilbanks[83] in Dade County (Miami), Florida, provides another illustrative account of Black, White, and Latino killings. This unprecedented study was the first to present information on murders by and of Cubans, the third-largest Latino group after Mexican Americans and Puerto Ricans.[84] Even though the ethnic group comparisons focused exclusively on 1980, they directed attention to a predominantly Latino city in the midst of profound demographic changes, largely spurred by several waves of Cuban immigrants fleeing political turmoil since 1960.[85] Most important was the finding that even though Latinos constituted the majority of all homicides in Miami, they were not over-represented relative to population size.[86] Again, Latino rates fell between those of Whites and Blacks.

A number of studies have examined homicide among several prominent ethnic groups in Miami, Florida. For example, although Mariel refugees were often portrayed by the media as high-rate killers, the empirical evidence demonstrated that they were not at either the "victim" or the "violator" level, and that in fact, after a few years, they were much less likely to be offenders than Miami's established Cubans.[87] In addition, despite a constant influx of Latino immigrants in the 1980s, Miami's homicide rates continued to decline, in particular among Latinos, and most often involved native African-American victims and offenders.[88] Finally, Martinez and Lee[89] found that Miami's Haitians and Latinos were underrepresented in homicide relative to group size, while African Americans were overrepresented, and in some cases the rate of homicide among the two immigrant groups was *lower* than that of non-Latino Whites (Anglos).

Consistent with earlier studies, the criminal involvement of immigrant groups varies considerably across cities. A good example of this variation is provided in a study of Latino homicide among El Paso's Mexicans and Miami's Cubans.[90] Despite the two cities' similar structural characteristics, such as employment, poverty, and so forth, Miami's Latino homicide rate was almost three times that of El Paso. In addition to city-specific characteristics such as Miami's older population, greater income inequality,[91] and possibly greater availability of guns, other local conditions shaped the comparatively high Cuban homicide rate. For example, Cubans settled in a more violent area of the country (southern Florida) than Latinos in El Paso, and this regional context may shape each group's involvement in homicide. Wilbanks[92] demonstrated that Miami's homicide trends mirror those for southern Florida generally, and that this area experienced a sharp rise in homicides before the arrival of thousands of Cuban refugees in the Mariel boatlift of 1980. Thus Miami's Latinos lived in a location experiencing higher levels of violence than El Paso's Latinos.

Just as important differences were revealed by the experiences of two Latino groups in the research described above, other studies also have examined within-group differences among ethnic groups.[93] Martinez and Lee[94] investigated Afro-Caribbean homicides in Miami and found that Mariel Cuban, Haitian, and Jamaican immigrants were generally less involved in homicide than natives. Comparing the early 1980s, when these groups first began arriving in Miami in large numbers, to 1990, the authors discovered a strong pattern of declining violence, especially for Jamaicans and Mariels, while Haitians continuously maintained an extremely low overall rate relative to the city total. As these immigrant groups grew in size, and had a lower proportion of young males, homicide rates rapidly dissipated. This finding suggests that contrary to key propositions of traditional social disorganization theory, rapid immigration may not create disorganized communities but may instead stabilize neighborhoods through the creation of new social and economic institutions.[95] The general conclusions of recent research on immigration and crime echo themes in earlier studies. Immigrants seem to be generally less involved in crime than similarly situated native groups in the small number of studies providing empirical evidence, despite the wealth of prominent criminological theories that provide good reasons for why this should not be the case (e.g., residence in disorganized neighborhoods, acculturation difficulties, and conflicts between cultural codes, to name a few). Furthermore, immigrant experiences vary greatly with local conditions, as illustrated by the comparison of Cubans in Miami and Mexicans in El Paso, and it is likely that these conditions shape criminal involvement to a larger degree than the cultural traditions of the groups themselves.

The 1987 UCLA Conference

While the Latino homicide studies just mentioned were important, these efforts as a whole have had relatively little impact on the manner in which government agencies and most individual researchers study the causes and extent of urban violence.[96] A notable exception was a 1987 research conference on violence and homicide in "Hispanic" communities conducted at the University of California, Los Angeles. While most of the presentations were descriptive in nature and focused on a variety of violence-related topics,[97] several specifically addressed the issue of homicide among Latinos. Because all of these reports had different methodologies, I will analyze each one individually.

The most elaborate of these, at least in terms of city size and theoretical consideration, was conducted by Margaret A. Zahn,[98] who presented a variety of findings related to Anglo, Black, and Latino homicide in 1978, including cases in nine large cities (Philadelphia, Newark, Chicago, St. Louis, Memphis, Dallas, San Jose, Oakland, and Ashton—the latter was a required code name for a Far West city). Together, these homicide incidents gave a good indication of where Latino victims and offenders fell in relationship to Blacks and Whites in a wide array of circumstances and regional context at a given time point.

The statistical evidence contained in the Zahn chapter stated that, in line with a host of previous research, Latino victim and violator rates were between those of Whites and Blacks. Specifically, the level of Latino killings was three to four times that of Whites and half that of Blacks. Several other findings also emerged: First, Latino male rates were several times that of White counterparts but much less than that of Blacks; second, Latina rates were almost the same as for White females, and the latter two were several times lower than for Black females; third, Latino male victims' and offenders' average age was lowest of all three ethnic groups; and fourth, Latinos were more likely to be killed by a friend or a stranger than in any other victim/offender relationship.

Margaret Zahn argued that while Latino economic deprivation (e.g., unemployment and poverty) corresponded with that of Blacks, strict structural or cultural approaches alone could not adequately explain the differences between groups with similar economic characteristics. Poverty was endemic in Latino communities, but homicides were lower than expected, given widespread low income and relatively high unemployment, which rivaled that of African Americans. Again, Zahn speculates that comparisons between recent and more established Latinos, as well as manner of reception in the United States (political or economic), might shed some light on their comparatively low homicide rate.

Other workshop contributors provided similar analyses of homicide among Latinos. In his five-state study using mortality data from 1979 to 1981, James A. Mercy[99] noted that homicide was one of the most important sources of death for foreign-born Latinos. In fact, homicide was the second leading cause of death for Mexicans and third among Cubans. Mercy produced valuable information on the extent of homicide, but moreover his ethnic comparison was one of the few to examine Latino group differences. Like Zahn, Mercy also emphasized that homicide among Latinos fell between that of Whites and Blacks, providing within and between ethnic group comparisons.

Richard Spence[100] reached conclusions at odds with those of other contributors, but his reference point varied from those of the other panelists. He discovered that along the Texas and Mexico border area "the homicide rates for Hispanics of all age groups in border counties is less than half that of Hispanics in nonborder counties" in the Lone Star State. He explained this phenomenon by contending that Latinos away from the border were socially isolated and did not have the same type of family and community support found in Mexico or in border counties.

Other analyses of Latino homicide in urban areas at the UCLA workshop ranged from systematic to anecdotal, but all were unanimous in finding that Latino rates fell within those of Whites and Blacks. Block, for example, discovered that in Chicago, the 1980 Latino victim rates fell between the White and Black rates, but again, Latino male rates (68.9) were closer to Black male levels (84.6) than Whites (15.3) per 100,000. Orlando Rodriguez also found very similar rates at the same time in New York City, with Latino, primarily Puerto Rican, male rates of 67.8 per 100,000 Latinos several times greater than for Whites (18.8) but one-third less than Black male rates (95.3). Nevertheless, the total Latino homicide rates followed parallel contours in Chicago and New York City.[101]

One potential explanation for the similarity in the Block and Rodriguez findings is that the two cities were in the throes of economic transformation. Valdez and Nourjah,[102] however, found comparable ethnic-specific figures in Los Angeles County, as did the other conference participants. Latino victim rates were two to three times higher than for Anglos but half that of Blacks in 1980. Overall, however, Valdez and Nourjah maintained that since 1970 the Latino homicide rate rose rapidly, and this shift increased the most for Latino males. Even with this noticeable upward spiral, the age and male-specific Latino rates peaked at levels far below those of Black counterparts.

Not everyone, however, maintained that Latino comparison to Blacks and Whites was the primary and most appropriate reference point. Cynthia Leyba[103] noted that Blacks and Native Americans had higher homicide rates than Latinos and Whites in Albuquerque, New Mexico. Again, the Latino rate was twice that of Whites, a third less than that of Native Americans, and three times lower than that of Blacks. She found, however, that gender comparisons were the most useful points of contrast. The Latino male rate was several times higher than for Whites, but the contrasts to the other two groups remained. Like Zahn, Leyba discovered that the Latina homicide rate was both low and in line with that of White and Native American females and that all three were substantially lower than for Black females.

Taken together, the various papers on Latino homicide issued by the UCLA workshop paint a consistent picture of killings among U.S. Latinos. The findings presented were, at the time, the best indicators of the extent and severity of Latino homicide: In most regions and areas, Latinos committed homicide and were victims at a level higher than the total population in general and Whites in particular. Moreover, the admittedly descriptive analyses usually supported the conclusion that factors influencing Blacks and Latinos, such as poverty and unemployment, might not influence both groups equally, even though this notion was never directly tested. But perhaps the most relevant aspect of these findings is that Latinos, heavily foreign-born, had rates of homicide much lower than that of similarly situated native-born Americans (African Americans and Native Americans), reminding us again that Latinos are not as homicidal as expected.

CONCLUSION

The bulk of empirical studies conducted over the past century have found that immigrants, and Latinos in general, are usually underrepresented in criminal statistics. There are variations to this general finding, and even though some studies treat Latinos as immigrants regardless of year of entry, these appear to be linked more to differences in structural conditions across areas where immigrants settle than to the cultural traditions of the immigrant groups. *Local context appears to be the central influence shaping the criminal involvement of both immigrants and natives, although in many cases immigrants seem more able to withstand crime-facilitating conditions than native groups.*

   Community contexts are described more vividly in the next chapter. As mentioned before, immigration changes in the 1980s and 1990s gave rise to massive population displacement within urban America and Latino communities. This cannot be attributed to any single external pressure or viewed as an aberration in the history of Latinos. Instead, it may be conceived as one part of an older history described in a body of literature that reminds us that crime is a constant in ethnic minority communities. To gain a deeper understanding of the background of Latinos and crime, we must go deeper into the conditions Latinos face. The roots of contemporary Latino violence may in fact be found in conditions established decades ago, even though the current results in many ways are similar to the old ones.

3. THE CREATION OF LATINOS
Local Context and Contemporary Crime

EVEN WITH THE GROWING Latino presence, many U.S. citizens are unaware of the roots of Latino immigration in a colonial empire constructed in the nineteenth and early twentieth centuries. Politicians and business interests perpetuated this period of U.S. territorial expansion, which laid the foundation for and "helped spark massive Latino immigration after World War II," leading to the creation of many contemporary Latino communities.[1] This growth was evident in many homes, schools, neighborhoods, voting booths, television networks, and even jails and prisons, as many noticed Spanish-language instructions for the first time in their lives and observed Latinos moving in next door or across the street.

Many Americans were concerned about these newcomers, and insecurity set in as images of Latinos as "barbarians at the gate invading our cities" and communities took hold.[2] The latest image is discussed in Juan Gonzalez's[3] introduction to *A History of Latinos in America*, where he describes "They saw images of Mexican street gangs in Los Angeles and Phoenix, Puerto Rican unmarried mothers on welfare in New York and Boston, Colombian drug dealers in Miami, or illegal Central American laborers in Houston and San Francisco. These immigrants, they were told in countless news reports, refused to assimilate, clung to their native language and culture, and were disproportionately swelling the ranks of the country's poor." In reaction, "law and order" politicians demanded tougher immigration laws and harsher sentences for those overstaying their welcome, even while hate crimes directed against immigrants swelled.[4] Yet, as the size of the Latino population skyrocketed, many thought Latino crime grew, and thought that Latino neighborhoods were dangerous places to live and visit. This chapter continues the complex saga of Latinos within the United States.

COMMUNITIES AND LOCAL CONDITIONS

A long history of political and military intervention and economic involvement has forged deep ties that bind Mexico, Cuba, and Puerto Rico to the United States.[5] Spanish-speaking settlers, missionaries, and *conquistadores* first established communities on the Rio Grande four hundred years ago, in the aftermath of the 1845 Mexican War and the Treaty of Guadalupe Hidalgo, when Mexico ceded her northern territories and residents and they became the southwestern portion and people of the United States.[6] Although separated by the new boundary, old Mexican communities in San Diego and El Paso continued to attract other Mexicans, and this appeal intensified over time as civil and economic strife dominated Mexico after 1910 and as the Southern Pacific and Santa Fe Railroads grew.[7] "Track gangs" required labor, resulting in continued northern migration for many males, in some cases for a few months and in others for several years. Gradually World War II drew manpower away from the agriculture industry, and *braceros,* or guest workers, were invited to enter the United States, work the fields, and sometimes stay during periods of economic growth. Many settled in and around the Mexican border; others moved farther north with the railroads, eventually landing in Chicago's stockyards and factories, and other points between.

As economic conditions improved in the United States, and as World War II ended and the baby boomers boomed, Spanish-speakers in other previously conquered and colonized areas were encouraged to enter *El Norte* (North America), where jobs and riches waited for these new "Americans" in the New York City barrios. The 1898 Spanish-American War garnered Puerto Rico and Cuba (and other areas), and between 1945 and 1965 hundreds of thousands of Puerto Ricans left the island and headed for New York City and Chicago.[8] Although citizens by birth, many Puerto Ricans found the "Promised Land" inviting and accommodating, but others discovered a hostile reception, poverty, and social isolation.[9]

While Puerto Ricans flew airplanes to the Far North, Cubans were landing only a couple of hours away. Shortly after Fidel Castro's revolution in 1959, many Cubans left, and started what many thought would be a short exile in Miami. Instead, Castro did not fall, and hundreds of thousands followed during the 1960s and 1970s. Early arrivals tended to be much more affluent than the later waves that followed, and although they were not rich, the early arrivals were more educated and skilled than the more recent immigrants were. Since 1980, Cuban newcomers raised under a Communist regime have been far less than prosperous, as noted in accounts on the *Marielitos* or Cuban refugees who left the Mariel Harbor in Cuba and arrived in Miami on boats in the summer of 1980. Recent arrivals, or *balseros,* who drifted toward Florida on crude rafts made of inner tubes in the 1990s, are also generally poorer than the earlier exiles. Nevertheless, Miami's Little Havana neighborhood had a ready social network that absorbed the continuous stream of Cubans, and at times welcomed Nicaraguans fleeing Castro's left-wing comrades in the 1980s. Other Latino areas in Miami grew, accepting an array of Latinos, none of whom resembled the "golden exiles" of the 1960s because they had grown up under Communist rule and were less educated than the first ones.

Where old Cubans lagged behind new ones was in failing to concern mainstream American society, the major exception being the Marielitos, who were soon stereotyped as dangerous Latinos, much like Mexicans and Puerto Ricans before them. We will see later in this book that if any single event contributed to the immigrant hypercriminal predator, it was the arrival of the refugees on the Mariel boatwave.[11] As Norman and Naomi Zucker[12] have noted, "Domestically, the watchword was control. Immigrants, refugees, asylum seekers, illegal entrants, all were lumped together in the public mind as opportunists trying to defraud a system that was 'out of control.' Election campaigns from the local to the presidential level would sound the alarm that Americans had lost control, were losing their country—to crime, to welfare, and the immigration. And the Mariel boatlift had come to symbolize all three."

While the Mariels symbolized a new era—one of a growing concern of immigrants and Latinos at large, and as stereotypes surrounding Mariel criminals increased—the public at large wanted to control these newcomers. Combined with a renewed effort to get "tough on crime" begun during the early 1980s, attempts to "protect the border" had an effect on the recognition and identification of Latinos in contemporary society. I now turn to this process—a clarification on who and what are Latinos.

LATINO IDENTITY

Extending the race and crime debate to include Latinos means that group recognition is based on ethnicity, not just race, so the context in which this definition occurs requires elaboration. An ethnic group is typically defined as people with a common history, features, and culture, who tend to interact and identify with others containing similar traits. Many scholars, social observers, and political commentators assume that Latinos have many of the characteristics used to portray *ethnicity* and permit *ethnic group* members to distinguish each other from individuals outside that group. However, the social and political construction of Latino identity merits attention, since some debate exists regarding the classification of Latinos: who they are, what that designation means and represents, and if they warrant recognition as a distinct ethnic group.[13] Are Latinos fundamentally different from Blacks and Whites? Or, as some claim, are group distinctions within the Latino population more pronounced than relative to Blacks and Whites?[14] While I do not intend to definitively answer these questions, it is necessary to address this issue before proceeding to the stated aims of this book.

First, it is important to note that official federal agencies used the term *Hispanic*—a designation widely used in the 1970s—to construct an identity for a heterogeneous group that consists of people who vary by skin color and national origin but have similar cultural and ethnic roots in twenty-three Spanish-speaking countries.[15] This government label is linked to Spain's centuries-old presence in the American hemisphere, but in the context of contemporary debates on ethnicity and race, its use has problematic political significance and other limitations according to those interested in constructing a pan-Latino identity. Others argue that the term *Latino* emerged as a "progressive alternative" to the government label, and that it is widely used in many urban areas where various Latino groups reside, which increases the likelihood of contact and group solidarity.[16] Thus the male and female terms "Latinos" and "Latinas" arose out of a collective identity initiated by federal bureaucrats, assisted in no small part by political and business interests.[17] Both interests—those motivated to redress the effects of past discrimination and deterring new forms of bias; and others, interested in marketing, serving, or representing one large Spanish-speaking audience—assert that this group existed and deserved separate classification.[18]

While there is some critical tone in the proceeding paragraph, there is also tremendous value in justifying the use of a "Latino identity" in contemporary America. Despite some differences, Latinos constitute a distinctive linguistic and cultural group, and clearly few other groups have dominated the prolonged wave of immigration in the manner that Latinos have since 1965. It is also clear that the "Latino intelligentsia" prefers this identifier and insists that it is the most precise label we have. My potential audience (professionals and students) is most comfortable with that designation as well.

Two things also are clear. Ethnic and racial identification is not a precise classification, even though the personal and political boundaries formed by skin color are clear to most people. Most Latinos, both native and foreign-born, choose national origin (e.g., Mexican, Puerto Rican, Cuban, etc.) over a panethnic identity.[19] As an example, I call myself ethnically "Latino" in my adopted hometown of Miami but consider my Latino ethnicity "Chicano" or "Mexican-origin" in my birthplace of Texas. I know many who consider themselves as ethnically Latino but also refer to themselves as "Puerto Rican" or "Cuban" when appropriate. Rodolfo de la Garza and colleagues[20] note in *Latino Voices: Mexican, Puerto Rican, & Cuban Perspectives on American Politics*, a volume drawn from a survey of political attitudes among the three largest Latino groups in forty metropolitan areas, that most "overwhelmingly prefer to identify in national-origin terms such as Mexican American, Puerto Rican, or Cuban." Whenever possible, I stress the Latino group identifier—Mexican, Puerto Rican, Cuban, Nicaraguan, Dominican, and so on.[21]

Many Latinos also avoid classifying themselves in strict White or Black racial categories, preferring the Latino term in lieu of traditional racial identifiers or, "Other Race."[22] As I just observed, skin color or American perceptions of race are not dichotomies for most Latinos. To illustrate the long history of Mexican "skin color," Diego Vigil[23] recently noted in *From Indians to Chicanos: The Dynamics of Mexican American Culture* the significance of issues surrounding racial varieties in colonial Mexico, a period when Spanish conquistadores were mingling with indigenous populations, producing "a hybrid race (Mestizos) representing a color spectrum from white to black, from European to native or African features. There were also new, heretofore unseen variations of color and physiognomic qualities." Vigil's account[24] emphasized the "different types and degrees of racial heritage" coming from the new breed that was neither Spanish nor Indian, but certainly a niche different from "peon Indians or African slaves." Therefore the Latin American and Caribbean concept of "race" is viewed as a continuum that captures various shades of color and physical appearances, with many or most somewhere between the U.S. racial dichotomy.[25] Latinos are an ethnic group rising out of contacts among Spanish settlers, indigenous residents, and slaves throughout the Americas. In sum, Latinos exhibit an array of skin color and physical traits that contrasts to U.S. notions of race; in fact, one common characteristic of most Latinos is a rejection of the strict racial classifications of White or Black.[26]

But parallels among Spanish-speakers in the Western Hemisphere outweigh the distinctions. All have a cultural experience created by a legacy of Spanish rule and the colonizing influences that profoundly shaped the history of Latin America and the Caribbean. Contemporary experiences also have been unkind. The presence and current social conditions of Puerto Ricans and Mexicans in the United States are rooted in the conquest of territory, political and economic domination, and historical encouragement of migration for cheap labor or Cold War propaganda purposes, among other reasons.[27] These events distorted the development of other Spanish-speaking countries within the sphere of U.S. influence and affected their settlement patterns and growth in ways that European immigrants never encountered.[28] Few non-Latino immigrants in the past or present have the common characteristic of experiencing a long-term and external political involvement in internal matters as Latinos, whose cultures have been influenced by U.S. policy in Latin America and the Caribbean.[29] Moreover, U.S. interference and domination in Spanish-speaking America, in turn, shaped development, limited growth, heavily affected conditions in their respective points of origin, and exacerbated movement to go abroad.[30]

Immigration also is an influential component of the Latino experience, and unlike with most other ethnic groups, it is impractical to ignore its impact on patterns of Latino urban crime. Not only does immigration influence the social, economic, and demographic position of Latinos, but also it is potentially confounded with other characteristics of crime in the United States, including urban decay.[31] In fact, proponents of immigration restriction label immigrants as a major cause of urban violence, pointing to recent riots as evidence. Immigrants also are linked to other social problems, including ethnic tensions such as widespread group conflict among ethnic minorities over low-paying jobs.[32] However, other than rare instances, little empirical support exists to sustain these popular notions.[33]

On the other hand, immigration reinforces the "cultural" attributes of Latinos by intensifying the use of Spanish, fueling the growth of a Spanish-speaking media actively portraying Latinos as a single entity, and shaping traditional notions of marriage and family. According to the previously mentioned work by de la Garza and colleagues,[34] Latinos are usually to some extent bilingual, or Spanish-dominant, with the smallest category speaking only English. The overwhelming majority are Catholic (but not necessarily religious), and most reside in highly segregated areas, rarely interacting with non-Latinos, while recent immigrants tend to live among older and more established ethnic group members. Levels of neighborhood segregation are high among Latinos, and it is difficult to find a large urban mass outside of a handful of states.[35]

Yet another defining Latino experience is economic disadvantage. Benigno Aguirre and Rogelio Saenz[36] in the article "A Futuristic Assessment of Latinos' Ethnic Identity" and others note how Latino workers, regardless of origin, have experienced a serious decline in income and poverty since 1978.[37] This deterioration hit all Latino groups hard, with Mexican-origin groups and Puerto Ricans usually the poorest of them all. However, despite the acclaimed Cuban entrepreneurial experience, much of that population now consists of *Mariels and Balseros*, who are far from well off in contemporary Miami.[38] The economic change coincided with a national slump in the economy throughout most of the 1980s, which in turn increased the scapegoating of Latinos, but also fortified the common ground among Latinos and contributed to a cohesive identity.[39]

The writings of Roberto Suro[40] complement this discussion of

Latino identity. As Suro[41] has put it in his widely publicized account *Strangers among Us: How Latino Immigration Is Transforming America*, Latinos comprise a distinct group bound by many similarities, acknowledging the diversity but contending that those contrasts pale in comparison to other groups. Take, for example, the Asian population, whose proportion of immigrants was higher (63.1 percent) than Latinos (35.8 percent) in 1990, but who were dwarfed by the sheer number of Latinos.[42] In fact, there were more *foreign-born* Latinos, over eight million, than the almost seven million *total* number of Asians and Pacific islanders.[43] Moreover, in San Diego, a city where Asians outnumber African Americans, the two largest Asian groups are Filipinos and Vietnamese, residing among a much older Chinese and Japanese population and representing a much greater variety of distinct cultures, languages, and social experiences than Latinos. The Asian social, economic, and cultural differences provide a stark contrast relative to Latino group differences, where Spanish is spoken regularly, Catholicism reigns, and work is routine but at poverty wages.

Some might argue that Latinos are much more comparable to Whites, or that Cubans are far too different from Mexicans, and that other Latino groups have more in common with African Americans or Caribbean Blacks. But in urban America, where crime and immigrants are concentrated, the economic conditions for Latinos in Miami and El Paso, for example, are *exactly* the same, the differences between heavily Cuban or Nicaraguan neighborhoods in Miami are relatively modest, and the socioeconomic similarities are profound across Latino groups. Latinos are poor but working, and are less crime-prone than expected, attacks by political commentators notwithstanding.

Thus I find that the use of "Latino" is essentially a proxy for Spanish-speaking groups with roots in the Americas. It refers to different groups in various contexts that could be primarily Cuban in Miami or Mexican in El Paso, Houston, and San Diego, with some variation in urban areas, including Chicago, where Puerto Ricans and Mexicans coexist. Latinos are a unique group shaped by a similar cultural experience largely unparalleled by other ethnic groups in the United States, and influenced by closeness to their country of origin and the Spanish-speaking media. Disagreements and distinctions aside, no other viable ethnic comparison exists, few options are available to distinguish this group from others, and so I find that this is the most useful term to apply. The Latino group differences discussed above are real, but little evidence exists that differences outweigh similarities or that distinctions influence broad trends in terms of crime and victimization, the areas I am most concerned with.

The Current Research Sites: Chicago, El Paso, Houston, Miami, and San Diego

While post-1980 immigration revitalized many urban poor communities and contributed workers for the service economy, it also reshaped the Latino population and fueled Latino poverty. As we see in table 3.1, in 1970 and 1980 the percent of Blacks living below the federal poverty rate was much higher than for Latinos, but those numbers have changed, and Latino poverty is now equal to or higher than that of Blacks. By 1995, for the first time a higher proportion of Latino than Black households live in poverty.[44] This change in economic status is a reflection of a long trend of declining incomes among Latino households, attributable in part to high levels of immigration.

TABLE 3.1
POVERTY RATES BY ETHNICITY IN THE UNITED STATES, 1970–95

	Percent Poor by Ethnic Group				
	1970	1980	1985	1990	1995
Black	33.3	31.0	30.0	31.0	29.0
Latino	22.2	25.0	28.0	26.0	31.0
Anglo	9.9	10.1	10.0	11.0	11.0

Source: U.S. Bureau of the Census as cited in Holmes 1996.

However, this is not to suggest that 1980, the starting point for this book and the beginning of the Latino immigration surge, was the high point of economic well-being for Latinos. In reality, the decade of the eighties did not start off well for urban Latinos, as many cities in this study illustrate. While Puerto Rican and Mexican neighborhoods in Chicago are now growing in terms of prominence and power, they do so in the wake of an economy decimated by a declining manufacturing industry and a subsequent loss of well-paying jobs requiring only hard work and few technical skills. As factories left Chicago in the 1970s and early 1980s, and in many ways left it in ruins, the oil industry bottomed out in Houston, leaving behind empty apartment complexes and vacant subdivisions of new houses. Gradually a new strand of heavily indigenous Central Americans, such as Mayans and Incans, joined an older Chicano community, simultaneously attracting recent Mexicans to "Space City" as the city rebuilt and eventually rebounded from the early 1980s oil bust.

Both Chicago and Houston rebounded from economic decline as the 1990s came to a close and as the diverse Latino communities continued to grow. Each city now sustains well over a million residents and a large Latino population. While those of Mexican origin comprise 13 percent of Chicago's population and 30 percent of Houston's, and were by far the largest and fastest-growing Latino group in both cities at the turn of the century, they are now mingling with a large community of non-Mexican Latinos. Puerto Ricans in Chicago and Salvadorans[45] in Houston comprise similar proportions of the local population—about 5 percent in 1990—and have formed distinct communities in and around the older, well-established Mexican barrios, but in some cases far away from the Mexican-origin residents.

If the 1980s were turbulent in Chicago and Houston, 1980 was an especially difficult year in Miami. No one could have foreseen that over the summer 125,000 people would flee Cuba through Mariel Harbor, moving toward southern Florida, and eventually settling in the Miami metropolitan area (Portes and Manning 1987). Even fewer could predict the consequences of absorbing the newcomers; much less anticipate the damaging stereotypes shaping the "Marielitos'" public image almost as soon as they landed in Miami. This unique episode in American immigration history cemented Miami's status and reputation as a predominantly Latino city and predated the massive Latino immigration wave hitting the rest of America (Portes and Stepick 1993: 21). As the 1980s progressed, the Mariels also accelerated the growth of the well-known Cuban neighborhood—Little Havana—beyond its original boundaries and fueled Cuban movement beyond the Miami City limits. While the Mariels replaced fleeing Whites, Nicaraguans and other Central American groups (Salvadorans and Hondurans), simultaneously escaping political chaos, moved in and gained a foothold, attracted by Miami's proximity to Latin America and the success of its Spanish-speaking entrepreneurs. But yet again, as the 1990s closed, Cubans and others are washing ashore in rafts, spelling the start of yet another immigrant Latino episode as the *Balseros* join the enclave, cementing Miami's image as a predominantly Latino city.

Latinos, however, have long dominated other cities such as El Paso, which has been primarily of Mexican origin since its founding four hundred years ago as *El Paso del Rio del Norte*, marking the beginning of the *Camino Real*, a travel route into the United States founded by Spanish explorers.[46] The new route into the United States for many Mexicans frequently starts, passes through, or ends in this Texas border city. This movement is not unusual, since El Paso has historically served as a major entry point to both Mexico and the United States, and has a well-established reputation as a dangerous and lawless place. Nevertheless, while daily border crossings are frequent and many travelers are quite poor, a mature and visible Latino working/middle class exists, wielding a growing influence that ebbs and flows at times in support of coethnics trying to cross the Rio Grande.

San Diego is yet another site with more than a million residents (like Chicago and Houston) examined in this book; it also is one of the oldest cities on the U.S./Mexican border and the seventh-largest city in the United States. Estimates place San Diego's Mexican-origin population between one-fifth and one-quarter of the city's total population. Some have resided in the downtown barrios for multiple generations, and have now been joined by recent arrivals. Much like in El Paso, Mexican crossings into San Diego also contributed to its reputation as a dangerous place for Mexicans and Whites in the 1980s and 1990s and a growing perception that local crime is linked to those newcomers. For example, thousands of border crossings occur each day in San Diego's San Ysidro barrio; many are tourists, but others are Mexican day laborers, or are employed in the informal economy as maids, baby-sitters, and gardeners. Regardless of nativity, people of Mexican origin currently live in and around the busiest entry point into the United States, and Spanish is widely spoken throughout the area, making it feel far removed from downtown San Diego, which is only a short tram ride away.

In sum, these five cities are diverse in terms of ethnic composition (Mexican, Cuban, Puerto Rican, other Latinos) and region of the country (Southwest, South, and Midwest). But each city is similar in that vibrant and visible Latino communities profoundly impact everyday life, reflecting the ongoing struggles that face the growing Latino population, including immigration, poverty, and violence.

Time Frame: Immigration and Youth Violence

Ruben Rumbaut, a renowned immigration researcher, reports that according to the U.S. Census Bureau, Latinos comprised 9 percent of the total U.S. population (or 22.4 million people) in 1990, an increase of 53 percent from the 14.6 million Latinos counted in 1980.[47] Much of the addition has been due to recent and swift immigration from Spanish-speaking countries in Latin America and the Caribbean. To place this new immigration in a larger perspective, consider that since 1980 half of the Mexican-origin population (the bulk of the country's Latino population); more than one-quarter of the Cuban-origin population; and most Salvadorans, Dominicans, Colombians, Guatemalans, Nicaraguans, Peruvians, and Hondurans have immigrated into the United States. There is no doubt that immigration radically transformed both the urban American landscape and the Latino population in countless ways—replacing poor native-born Americans in center cities, providing cheap labor in rural and suburban areas, and extending the boundaries of settled Latino barrios and enclaves. But again, despite this rapid increase, surprisingly, relatively little is known about this potential influence on Latino crime.

My critique of previous research notwithstanding, this book demonstrates that solid data on these matters are difficult, but not impossible, to obtain.[48] Information on shifts in Latino crime involvement are even more scarce, but if any group should be affected by an influx of immigrants and crime it would be this one, especially in terms of the population level. The key question is whether immigrants contribute a disproportionate amount of crime beyond what we would expect from native populations with similar demographic characteristics.

Despite the data difficulties confronting researchers, a recent study attempted to concentrate on social and economic issues involving Latinos and other ethnic minority group members. A table in *Changing America: Indicators of Social and Economic Well-Being by Race and Hispanic Origin*, a book prepared by the Council of Economic Advisers for the President's Initiative on Race, provides some perspective on how Latino homicide may differ, along with several other criminal justice topics, from other ethnic groups.[49] In this table, 1985 through 1995 national rates of Latino homicide victimization[50] were estimated from death certificates forwarded to the National Center for Health Statistics

(NCHS). These data are based on the cause of death and include killings resulting from legal intervention such as police shootings or other excusable homicides (i.e., self-defense) not typically included in police homicide data. However, the data are limited in that no information is available on the victim-offender relationship or the motivation behind each killing. Furthermore, this information is usually not readily available below the state level, at least from the NCHS, and does not allow easy linkage to valuable information on social and economic conditions.

These shortcomings aside, the recent wave of immigrants (overwhelmingly Latino) appears *not* to have affected rates of Latino homicide, one of the most serious crimes and the one for which we have the most reliable data. As we will see in later chapters, theory and popular wisdom suggest that immigrants should be disproportionately involved in crime.[51] The trends reported in figure 3.1, however, show that Latino homicide victim rates remained stable nationwide with some very minor fluctuations, despite a massive increase in Latino immigrants and the overall total number of immigrants (Latino and non-Latino) in the 1988 through 1994 period.

While the figures provided do not offer a causal link, they are highly suggestive of the connection, or lack thereof, between immigration and crime. As we will see in the next chapter, scholars who study this issue stress that the relationship between immigrants and border crime is far from clear.[52] Nevertheless, the findings in figure 3.1 countered the widespread belief that violence was high as a result of more "illegal aliens" crossing into the United States, spreading crime, fighting over drug markets, and increasing gang activity along the path into the new destination.[53]

Latino immigrants had moved north to work in the service sector, and they were looking for steady jobs. The presence of violent crime, however, was not as immediate a concern in the everyday struggle to live in the United States for many Latinos. A constant deterioration in the economic and social conditions during the past two decades in Latin America caused millions of workers to leave rural areas and migrate to major cities and beyond their national border.[54] Add to this unstable economic mix a rise in dangerous political conditions, especially exposure to official violence from left- and right-wing death squads, and it is easy to see the allure of the American dream growing in many minds. Adjustment to the formal and informal job market probably proved easier

FIGURE 3.1

TOTAL AND LATINO IMMIGRANT COUNTS BY
LATINO HOMICIDE RATE, 1984–96

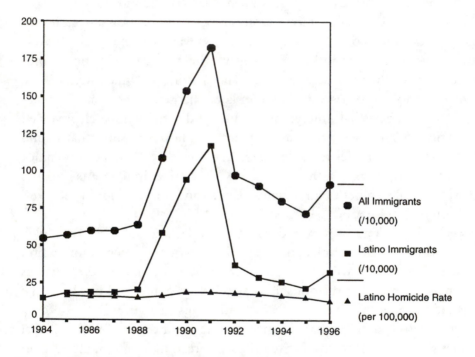

Note: Based on research by the author. The immigration figures are reported by the U.S. Immigration and Naturalization Service (1997, 1987); homicide victim rates are based on data from the National Center for Health Statistics as cited in *Changing America* 1999. This figure was originally published in "On Immigration and Crime" by Martinez and Lee 2001b: 506.

than participation in and exposure to crime, because life always was rougher and more violent in the home country.

Contemporary Crime in Context

It is also important to point out that as the presence of Latinos in the post-1979 United States became more noticeable, and as the economy fell, public commentary on immigration increasingly called attention to Latino crime. On the one hand, immigration alarmists, politicians, and right-wing journalists complain that too many crime-prone immigrants are entering the United States.[55] The argument goes: Spanish-speaking "criminal aliens" are a growing presence in the criminal justice system, requiring legislation to impede continued immigration, control immigrant criminals, and prevent further crime.[56] Former Colorado governor Richard Lamm, in a well-publicized book *The Immigration Time Bomb*, was among the first politicians to charge that Latino immigrants, especially Mariel Cubans in Miami, were responsible for a rise in crime and thwarted efforts to assimilate into American society, among other problems.[57] Lamm[58] wrote: "As far as we are from solving our own crime problem, we cannot afford to ignore the lawlessness that comes with the breakdown of our borders. Our immigration policies are exacerbating our national epidemic of crime. The most striking recent example of that lawlessness was the 1980 Mariel boatlift. Almost all of the 127,000 Cuban illegal immigrants in the Mariel boatlift will be given special treatment and consideration for permanent resident alien status, yet there is good evidence that 40 percent of them were criminals or had histories of criminal behavior or of mental illness."

Although Lamm never provided evidence to substantiate his claims, other than quoting a few horror stories or interviews with officials in places where few Mariels resided, the image of the latest Latino menace soon proliferated in the media and public imagination, and local anti-immigrant reactions moved from fears about Cubans in Miami to intensifying concerns in relation to Mexicans moving across San Diego. Juan Gonzalez's book *A History of Latinos in America* describes how the rise of nativist politicians and radio talk show hosts contributed to White vigilantes striking out at Mexican immigrants to emphasize their exasperation with "out of control" immigration.[59] Gonzalez notes how "Vigilante movements like 'Light Up the Border' formed, in which groups of citizens living in Southern California gathered at night to shine their car headlights across the border and stop Mexicans from crossing illegally. In some cases, groups of white supremacists took to attacking immigrants," he recalls.[60] But despite the prevailing wisdom spread by pundits and writers that high levels of "immigrant crime" are a routine and unavoidable product of immigration, scholars rarely produce any systematic evidence of this assumed social problem.[61]

This imagery has profound consequences for recent immigrants who are labeled as crime-prone, and consistently viewed in public opinion polls as burdens to society.[62] When asked whether specific immigrant groups have "been a good thing for the country," only a small percentage of Americans (in no case more than 25 percent) hold favorable opinions toward Mexicans and Cubans. In contrast, European immigrants, including English, Irish, and others from the first wave of immigration, are generally viewed at least twice as favorably as the recent immigrant groups. For example, 45 percent of respondents in 1995 rated the Irish favorably, the European group with the lowest rank.[63]

These assumptions and attitudes have important consequences. As noted, immigration critics claim that the U.S.-Mexican border is not only a dangerous area harboring foreign-born criminals but also is in the midst of a growing wave of violent crime shaped by drug traffickers and fueled by a widespread violent gang culture, including native-born Latinos.[64] Public anxiety about this region is reflected in the use of military patrols and aggressive INS initiatives designed to control the border and to prevent criminal aliens who were widely believed to be contributing to local crime from entering the United States.[65] Public anxiety also is heightened by the publication of books such as Thomas Muller's *Immigrants and the American City* (1993), which quotes anecdotal evidence provided by some writers in California communities suggesting that immigrants, especially Mexicans, were the primary contributors to high crime rates in and around Southern California cities. It is important to note that Muller does *not* suggest that crime is a routine cost of immigration, but demonstrates that others routinely associate immigrants with crime, even though little evidence exists that immigrants are involved in crime more than the native-born.

In response to the immigrant Latino criminal stereotype, the INS has deported thousands of legal residents, most of whom had minor violations. Again, according to Juan Gonzalez,[66] a "dragnet appears to be increasingly directed at Latino immigrants. In 1997, the INS deported or excluded more than 110,000 aliens, most of them for past criminal convictions, and almost double the number removed in 1996. Latinos from eight countries comprised 90 percent of those 110,000. The disparity in treatment of Latinos can be seen when we compare how the agency handles Canadians. The INS estimates there are 120,000 illegal Canadians residing here, the fourth-largest group of illegals, and 2.7 million Mexican. Yet, in 1996, only 2,057 illegal Canadians were apprehended and repatriated at the U.S. border, compared to 1.5 million Mexicans."

This movement at the border heightened concern about potential threats to U.S. safety and initiated a series of draconian responses by the federal government, including military patrols on the "out of control" border area.[67] The image of losing control of our border resulted in greater INS funding and tighter security. Border police have been beefed up to record levels, INS interdictions have grown, and the larger numbers of agents resulted in more sophisticated surveillance technology. Still, it is not clear if immigration has been slowed. Certainly it has not stopped.

Again, it is worthwhile to mention the *consequences* of these policies in terms of increased police shootings and the exacerbation of danger at the border. The American Friends Service Committee (AFSC) reports persistent Border Patrol shootings and the use of hollow-point, expanding-type bullets to shoot migrants suspected of throwing rocks at them, many running from agents back to Mexico or actually pulled down from the fence, resulting in injury or killing of dozens of Mexicans on the California border over the past two decades.[68] This is not to mention the repeated illegal searches of private property that affect immigrants and natives alike and "dramatic increases in human rights abuses" by Border Patrol agents.[69] In a recent annual report, the AFSC notes racial profiling of citizens, such as speaking accented English, at INS entry points continue and "U.S.-citizen Latinos/as report being detained, searched, insulted, humiliated, incarcerated for long periods of time or actually deported." Finally, it documents a "dramatic increase in hate crimes against [Mexican] migrant workers over the last three years" in northern San Diego and notes "dozens of assaults, beatings, shootings and killings by roving hate groups, snipers, teenage hoodlums, gangs" and Marines from nearby Camp Pendleton.[70]

Even with the concern of "illegal" immigration, nowhere was the impact of ethnicity and crime more evident than in the age/gender linkage. In the late 1980s, social scientists and policymakers were using the metaphor "youth violence epidemic" to describe an event that hit urban America's male youths hard, in particular African Americans, who experienced record-high violent victim rates connected to activity in the crack cocaine market.[71] Many scholars assumed similarly high levels for young Latino males, as reflected in the current focus on crimes committed by and against ethnic minorities, a function of a growing class of "superpredators," primarily young minority males (presumably), engaged in wanton destruction across urban America.[72]

Similar notions were applied to Latinos, and in fact many Latino males were stereotyped as drug/gang activity-prone, and the popular media portrayed the resurgence of gang-related behavior in Southern California and other urban areas as a "contagious" process spreading throughout the country.[73] The media routinely depicted drive-by shootings as common events in Latino communities, the appearance of Chicano gangs proliferated in television shows and movies, and pundits warned about the latest menace to American society.[74] These depictions had severe consequences, contributing to political responses advocating longer and harsher sentences to incarcerate these "dangerous predators," but with little systematic evidence of high Latino violence.[75]

Contrary to this imagery, the Latino homicide rate from 1985 to 1995 presented in table 3.2 remained relatively flat, not only during a period of intense immigration into the United States but also during the midst of record-high levels of homicide among Black youths and young adults in the late 1980s and early 1990s. It is important to emphasize that despite exposure to decaying social and economic conditions; the presumed upheaval wrought by immigration; residing in cities and neighborhoods influenced by drug trafficking and gang violence; and the implication that the Latino homicide rate should have rapidly risen, these factors did not necessarily shape Latino homicide trends. In fact, at least two interesting points emerge in this table. First, the highest Latino homicide victim rate (16.5 per 100,000) in 1990 was in line with the 1985 and 1995 rate for Latinos (not to mention that White rates were going down as well), despite massive immigration. If immigration contributes to crime, it should have during this period, and it should have dramatically pushed Latino homicide rates upward. A glance at the three time points confirms that is not the case. Furthermore, even though conservative journalists and political observers clamored to say that minority males had become criminal elements in society, and that intraracial killings reigned, evidence for high levels of Latino killings was less than persuasive.

Another important point can be made in table 3.2. Ethnic group differences are further illustrated by a comparison of the Latino homicide rate to Anglo (non-Latino Whites) and (non-Latino) Black killings. At each time point, Black homicide rates are the highest of all groups, with Latinos tending to fall in the middle. Black rates were usually two to two and a half times that of Latinos. In contrast, Latino rates were typically three to four times that of Whites. These findings suggest that Latino homicides have unique qualities that justify study apart from general rates, and should be given the same attention as that shown Black and White homicide rates. It also suggests that the homicide epidemic might not have hit Latinos as hard as similarly situated ethnic minority groups.

TABLE 3.2
HOMICIDE RATES BY ETHNICITY IN THE UNITED STATES, 1985–95

	Rates per 100,000 Resident Population		
	1985	1990	1995
Black	29.0	39.9	32.5
Latino	16.1	16.5	14.9
Anglo	4.6	4.3	3.7

Source: National Center for Health Statistics, as cited in *Changing America* 1998.

All of these empirical points taken together introduce doubt on the popular images of Latinos as criminals. The Latino homicide rate is higher than that of Whites, but not as high as would be expected given that their social and economic conditions rival those of African Americans (recall table 1.1). For this reason, scholars seek further evidence of patterns, trends, and causes that are often masked in traditional White or Black crime classification schemes.[76] Unfortunately, Latinos are now part of a national discussion on race and crime that is not based on systematic data on the extent and severity of Latino homicide. The lack of influence that the currently limited scholarship has had in determining policy, informing policymakers, and refuting stereotypes suggests that Latinos rarely influence these processes and typically are ignored.

On a more theoretical level, the distribution of Latino crime requires an explanation that takes into account the question of location—that is, the unique situations surrounding Latino killings in specific areas. More precisely, while homicides are mostly concentrated in the center of cities, Latino homicides are not randomly distributed across all urban neighborhoods, but focused in particular barrios. This fact is especially important to note for certain types of homicide, in particular those fueled by youths, drugs, and gangs, requiring us to move beyond earlier research by directly looking at where these incidents occur and in which urban Latino communities they are located.

In closing, to sort out the effects of ethnicity on crime, this book will next introduce a number of spatial techniques and evidence to refine and illustrate this point and to complete the story of Latino communities in context and homicide. In the next two chapters I will draw from specific Latino neighborhoods to explore unique barrio and enclave formations, distinct spatial patterns, and unique homicide concentrations, and will describe their significance in these Latino communities.

4. THE ORIGINS OF LATINO COMMUNITIES

THE COHORT OF RESEARCHERS who wrote throughout the pre–World War II decades about the daily circumstances facing European immigrants and Black migrants in urban American communities would have been surprised that Latino newcomers are now experiencing somewhat "favorable" aspects of everyday life.[1] As George J. Sanchez[2] put it, "Their work emphasized the sharp discontinuities between traditional . . . relations in Old World peasant villages and the life immigrants encountered in modern, industrial cities after migration." Thus pioneering studies found exposure to crime and criminal involvement in immigrant communities to be an unfortunate but expected outcome of the foreign-born migrants' irrefutable break with their past, and a consequence of living in a new and hostile environment.

Yet it is unclear if Latinos and Latino communities defy or exemplify the crime-prone or high-crime characterization in twenty neighborhoods drawn here from the five cities under study. Like other ethnic and immigrant groups, Latinos who settled in the United States often chose specific cities and communities previously settled by their compatriots. Many neighborhoods were populated by established Latinos, some families several generations old, others a couple of decades; almost all, however, were products of an earlier migrant stream. While violence was routine in many places and many residents were potentially at risk for a number of urban problems, economic opportunities were relatively abundant and political stability reigned in the United States more so than in the immigrants' home country, both at the turn of the twentieth century and the start of the current one.[3] Where the two eras diverge is in the founding of Latino communities. I contend that they now create a buffer zone against crime despite living conditions as dilapidated as in any other impoverished community.

Just as the twentieth century ended as it began—researchers debating the consequences of immigration in urban communities—I now examine the dynamics of crime in Latino neighborhoods. Communities are important units of analysis for a number of reasons. First and foremost, the large and distinct Latino communities in each city provide an opportunity to discuss many issues in greater depth than is possible with larger aggregations. For example, criminological research since the pioneering work of Shaw and McKay[4] notes that the concentration of crime in "low-income areas near downtown" is a prominent and even routine center city characteristic, and the stability of this finding holds in this chapter.[5] Moreover, ethnic minority composition and high levels of immigration also were enduring features of the community characteristics noted by the Chicago School of Sociology at the turn of the twentieth century.[6]

However, the "immigration effect" in Latino communities is practically impossible to replicate in White and Black communities.[7] Immigrants potentially increase poverty and low levels of education, but also contribute to labor force participation. Latinos are poor but working—an acute difference relative to other ethnic groups. Nevertheless, my primary concern is with comparing and contrasting the community level conditions of urban Latinos to neighborhood violent crime such as homicide.

Furthermore, there are working/middle-class Latino neighborhoods, or at least middle-class communities with a large Latino presence near poor Latino communities, that also are included in this chapter. These are not perfectly matched to White middle-class communities, the most valid comparison group in those cities where these circumstances exist, for one reason: Middle-class White communities are geographically distant from urban poor areas (as in the case of San Diego), regardless of ethnic composition, and relatively well-off Latinos reside closer to poorer members of their communities than Whites.[8] Still, the five-city data are extended to include some working- and middle-class Latino areas.

Even though the twenty selected Latino communities are at times quite different from each other in ethnicity, such as Mexican, Puerto Rican, Cuban, or mixed Latino presence, many similarities arise in socioeconomic conditions, including high poverty, lack of educational attainment, political powerlessness and the like, which reflect the obstacles many ethnic minorities endure in urban America. Relative to the surrounding city characteristics, destitute circumstances abound in all of these Latino communities at a much higher level. An implication of this history of settlement and current conditions is that the ingredients contributing to high violent crime patterns, especially homicide, exist in these neighborhoods.

BARRIO/ENCLAVE FORMATION: THE CREATION OF LATINO COMMUNITIES

Even with the considerable earlier settlement history for Latinos through annexation and incorporation in the Southwest, their initial large-scale entry into urban American society occurred almost simultaneously with the arrival of European immigrants in the early 1900s.[9] The latter entry, of course, was a well-documented movement into the northeastern region or through Ellis Island and into the Midwest.[10] Historians have described the abandonment of rural European roots, the grueling voyage across the Atlantic Ocean, and difficult integration into American society experienced by many immigrants.[11] Others have demonstrated the severe consequences of immigration in Chicago, New York, and Philadelphia, arguing that population increases, the growth of urban poverty, and gang activities were commonly shared experiences. Indeed, studying the growth of urbanization and immigration gave rise to American sociology.

Not surprisingly, most historical writings on immigrants were influenced by European movement and emphasized acculturation into urban American communities that provided serious social and economic obstacles. Mexican residents also were exposed to these conditions in many rural and urban areas. Latinos were largely relegated to unskilled work in the Southwest, and settlement conditions for them were less than ideal. Many Latinos, initially exclusively of Mexican origin, faced an array of social problems beyond low pay, including slumlike housing; unhealthy living and working conditions; and a consistent pattern of social, economic, and legal discrimination.[12]

TABLE 4.1
INITIAL BARRIO/ENCLAVE FORMATION

City	Time Frame and Community
Chicago	Mexican, 1916 (Hull House and Stockyards)
	Puerto Rican, 1950 (Lincoln Park)
El Paso	1900, Chihuahuita (El Segundo)
Houston	1910s, Second Ward (El Segundo)
Miami	1960, Little Havana (Latin Quarter)
San Diego	1920s, Logan Heights (Barrio Logan)

Sources: Taylor 1932: 27; Padilla 1987: 78–79; Camarillo 1979: 209; Garcia 1981: 130; Rodriguez 1993: 104; Garcia 1996: 86.

Many Anglos, or non-Latino Whites, because of fear, hatred, and/or antipathy, sought to avoid these "aliens" and hoped to eventually control or at least constrain them.[13] David Montejano,[14] for example, in *Anglos and Mexicans in the Making of Texas, 1836–1986,* describes the repression of Mexican labor on southern Texas farms: "Horsewhipping, chains, armed guards, near-starvation diets, to name a few of the props involved, portray the more brutal size of labor coercion. Vagrancy laws, local pass systems, and labor taxes point to a more institutionalized dimension. The variety—even ingenuity—of these practices suggests a complex patchwork of exploitation. Clearly these diverse responses to the problem of Mexican mobility all point in the same direction— toward regulation of movement." Still others hoped to restrict further movement into the United States by asserting that a new problem would arise if Mexican growth continued. Historian David Gutierrez,[15] in his book *Walls and Mirrors,* quotes from a 1930 report presented to the House Committee on Immigration and compiled by Vanderbilt University economist Roy L. Garis where a representation of Mexicans is noted as: "These people sleep by day and prowl by night like coyotes, stealing anything they can get their hands on, no matter how useless to them it may be. Nothing left outside is safe unless padlocked or chained down," thus providing further evidence that preventing continued growth and controlling the new ethnic group was necessary to avoid urban decay. Their unfamiliarity with American social structures and inability to speak English made many of them victims of exploitation by coethnics and others.[16] Unacquainted with the local geography and unable to move about freely in their new cities, the new Latinos searched for accommodations in an area where others faced the same obstacles and where Spanish was typically spoken.[17]

Although Latinos had long lived in the southwestern United States, some settlers remained near the point of entry and joined other coethnics in the El Paso and San Diego areas, appealing alternatives to Mexico for many Mexican immigrants.[18] This flow continued unimpeded for two decades as American employers wooed Mexican labor into the Southwest and beyond.[19] The importation of Mexicans proved pivotal in the formation of barrios across urban America. (See table 4.1.)[20]

San Diego

Many Mexican immigrants chose San Diego as a permanent home since it contained an old Mexican-origin population and straddled the border.[21] Most of these immigrants clustered into a handful of areas centered in and around the downtown area known as Logan Heights, off Broadway, between the piers on Harbor Drive and Twenty-eighth Street (see figure 4.1).[22] Logan Heights attracted Mexican residents (and African Americans) as early as the 1920s, in part because of cheap housing and access to industries on the waterfront. By 1950 the western edge of Logan Heights moved near the harbor, evolving into the Mexican-dominant neighborhood now known as Barrio Logan, gradually assuming the characteristics of a ghetto—majority minority; extremely poor; and dominated by heavy industrial sites, including shipbuilding firms, chemical storage, and waste-recycling plants.

Others settled in what is now the border portion of the city.[23] Current residents of San Ysidro have adapted to life on the border, crossing into Tijuana, Mexico, frequently or daily. In fact, according to Herzog,[24] routine contact with border crossers into and out of Mexico has been a neighborhood characteristic since the 1920s, when gambling casinos, racetracks, strip joints, bars, and breweries enticed Americans across the border. The community boomed after U.S. business interests invested in Tijuana and housing was built for their workers. Americans actually initiated the early and routine border crossing, shuttling back and forth to Tijuana daily and returning to U.S. soil at night. However, this interest was short-lived. After the demise of Prohibition and the nationalization

FIGURE 4.1
San Diego Latino Neighborhoods

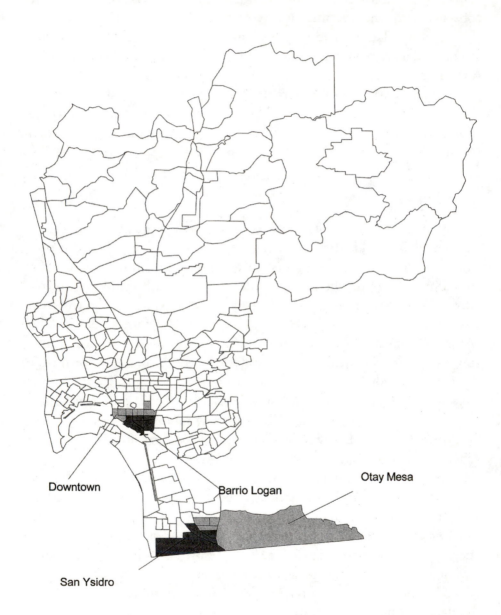

of foreign-owned properties in Mexico, the boom in San Ysidro subsided and the area reverted to its previous rural isolation.[25]

El Paso

Despite a history of ethnic tension and racial repression in Texas, the Mexican-origin population was able to maintain some semblance of power and authority in a few predominantly Latino cities along the Mexican border. In El Paso, the early 1900s found Mexican *patrones* or bosses acting as brokers and delivering political votes, labor, and the services of poorer, less-educated urban constituents to Anglo bosses.[26] In exchange, *patrones* provided various forms of assistance (e.g., emergency loans, etc.) throughout the year to working-class Mexicans, who, in turn, voted as instructed, consumed services, and settled in what eventually became one of the first barrios.[27]

These transactions entailed both costs and benefits. For example, many Mexicans avoided direct contact or rarely interacted with Anglos and isolated themselves in the segregated barrios of Chihuahuita or El Segundo, continuing to live everyday life much as they had since annexation (see figure 4.2). This strategy created a process of "community formation" that strengthened Mexican neighborhoods and prevented the community erosion or ethnic disintegration that many Anglos sought.[28] As might be expected, from this perspective the new Anglo society and other factors beyond their control forced Latinos into greater social disadvantage or, by contrast, Latinos self-segregated into these barrios. The problems barrio residents faced eventually proved difficult to overcome.[29]

Houston

Not all of the Mexican immigrants stayed in the United States; a few eventually returned to Mexico.[30] Most Mexican-origin residents, however, replenished older barrios or formed new ones. Houston, also known as "Space City," provides yet another twist in the story of Latino settlement. For example, the Mexican neighborhood of *Segundo Barrio* (Second Ward) emerged in a city rooted in a Confederate South tradition that was embedded in Jim Crow laws governing race relations between Whites and Blacks (see figure 4.3).[31] The barrio, originally settled

FIGURE 4.2
El Paso Latino Neighborhoods

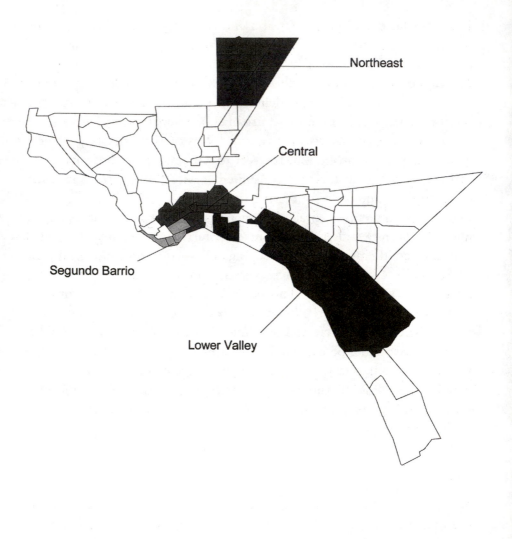

FIGURE 4.3
HOUSTON LATINO NEIGHBORHOODS

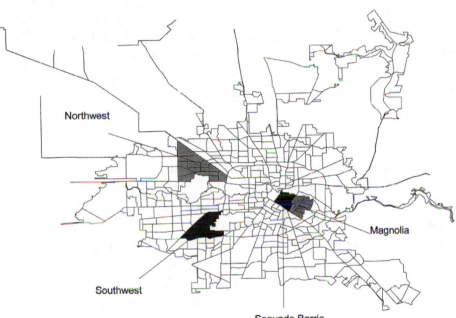

by European immigrants, sprouted in the 1910s even though the city itself had rarely accommodated those of Mexican origin.[32] As the railroads flourished and Houston grew, workers from nearby Texas communities and northern Mexico were attracted to the small *colonia*.[33]

The barrio blossomed as the neighborhood grew (fueled by civil strife in Mexico) and newcomers were absorbed into the local labor market. A few years later (and similar to San Diego), shipbuilding industries attracted thousands of Tejanos and Mejicanos to jobs two miles away from Segundo Barrio, and the Magnolia *colonia* emerged on the ruins of yet another neighborhood originally settled by White immigrants. Magnolia flourished as the ship channel and surrounding industries provided routine work, but again, with low pay and cheap housing. The Second Ward and Magnolia neighborhoods were permanent parts of Houston's landscape throughout the Great Depression, but eventually formed the foundation of Latino growth to other areas in the city.[34]

Chicago

If contemporary Latino Chicago was incorporated as a separate city it would be one of the largest in the United States—more than half a million Latino residents in 1990. In terms of sheer numbers and size, four Latino neighborhoods—Logan Square, Humboldt Park, West Town, and Pilsen[35]—comprise the bulk of the local Latino population and the heart of the Latino community (see figure 4.4).[36]

These areas are familiar to immigration scholars, since Chicago has long been known for its large and distinct ethnic and immigrant communities.[37] In recent years their racial and ethnic composition has changed dramatically (like elsewhere) as White ethnics moved to the suburbs and Latinos moved in, sometimes from older, adjacent Latino communities or directly from Mexico and Puerto Rico.[38] Despite this population succession and expansion, however, many of the same geographical boundaries still define residential concentrations of various racial and ethnic groups.[39]

Pilsen is within the officially defined neighborhoods of South Lawndale and Lower West Side, a community designation that dates back over one hundred years, when European immigrants dominated the local landscape. In fact, Taylor[40] notes that the current barrios were settled

FIGURE 4.4
CHICAGO LATINO NEIGHBORHOODS

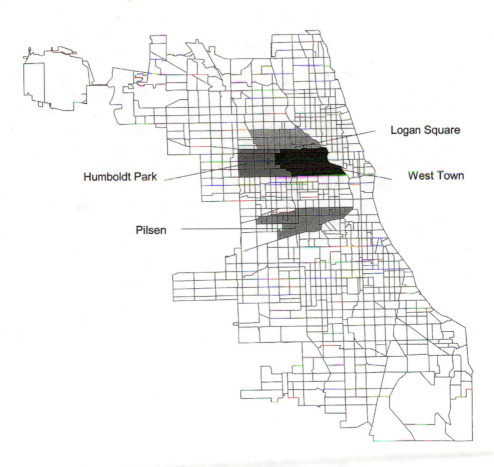

after those of Mexican origin initially moved into the Hull House and "Back of the Yards" areas near downtown Chicago. With time and gentrification the Mexican newcomers moved farther out and closer to work, creating one of the largest barrios outside the Southwest, which is now connected to the predominantly Mexican neighborhood known as the Heart of Chicago and treated as a large community.[41]

The factors that contributed to the emergence of Mexicans in the Southwest in the early 1900s later produced significant population changes in Chicago's Latino community during that time.[42] After World War II, a large group of Puerto Ricans moved from the island to labor in Chicago's manufacturing industries.[43] This was not a fortuitous event. The island and mainland agencies cooperated in identifying areas with temporary labor shortages and encouraged many Puerto Ricans to settle within those boundaries.[44] These circumstances were duplicated in the service sector as private households sought domestics and laborers from the island. Although Puerto Ricans are U.S. citizens, the basis and background of Puerto Rican movement from abroad and subsequent exploitative employment in Chicago have paralleled the Mexican work experience.[45]

For many Puerto Ricans, the near northwest side was soon chosen as a permanent home.[46] According to Felix Padilla,[47] West Town, Humboldt Park, and Logan Square have historically been the city's Puerto Rican barrios.[48] Proximity to work, public transportation, and cheap housing were important influences in anchoring the *Boricuan* barrios. But the neighborhoods have recently assumed a pan-Latino characteristic, and a substantial number of native and foreign-born Mexicans, as well as Latinos from the Caribbean and Central America, moved into adjacent neighborhoods from abroad.[49] Taken together, these neighborhoods form the foundation of one of the largest pan-Latino areas in the country.[50]

Miami

These settlement stories are not meant to imply consistency in the manner in which Latinos were lured to the mainland. Not all came through the Mexican border or from Puerto Rico. Direct Cuban immigration to Miami was a notable Latino exception.[51] The "Golden Exiles" fled Communist rule more than forty years ago, and many, if not most,

FIGURE 4.5
MIAMI LATINO NEIGHBORHOODS

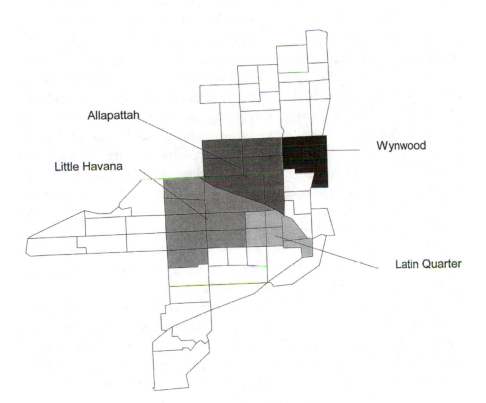

assumed a swift return to Cuba.[52] Hindsight proved them incorrect, and since additional Cuban immigrants were eventually concerned primarily with fleeing political despair and reuniting with family members, Miami was typically the only destination of interest.[53] Most exiles settled in Miami's neighborhoods, were accepted as "refugees," and absorbed into community life immediately after processing. (See figure 4.5.)[54]

This is not surprising, since proximity to Cuba, successful coethnics, a welcoming local community, and an accommodating federal government made Miami an attractive destination.[55] It had a small Cuban community even before the 1959 revolution, but many moved into Miami throughout the 1960s in one of the first of several waves.[56] Familiarity with the area, cheap housing, and special accommodation by the 1965 Cuban Refugee Act made life and adjustment somewhat easier than for other newcomers.[57] Most Cuban exiles settled in the Little Havana area southwest of downtown Miami. This "ethnic enclave" had long contained a small Cuban community, businesses serving the exiles, affordable housing, and access to adjacent downtown Miami.[58] Much like today in other central business districts, the immigrant newcomers revitalized the dilapidated business area on Calle Ocho and set up restaurants, *bodegas,* factories, bars, and theaters that continued to attract Cubans throughout the 1960s and 1970s.[59]

Moreover, the unique settlement patterns for Cuban immigrants were somewhat specific to Miami.[60] As Latino settlement persisted and as the character of the Cuban migration stream changed from "exiles" to "immigrants" and became more permanent, Little Havana expanded and the Cuban population increased to the point that throughout the 1970s and 1980s Miami was increasingly identified as a Latino-dominated city. According to the 1990 census, Cubans made up the largest ethnic group in spite of a growing middle class that had moved beyond the city limits, and the addition of a large Nicaraguan community adjacent to Little Havana. Many continued to flee a totalitarian country, join family members, and search for a better life in southern Florida throughout the 1980s and 1990s. But as we have seen, the origins of this enclave are atypical compared to the circumstances confronting other Latino communities and their residents.

Ethnic Concentration

Given that Latino settlement patterns are different from those of Blacks and Whites, an analysis of Latino communities requires consideration of Latinos separately from other ethnic groups. Within-Latino group differences also should be taken into consideration, since Latino settlement did not follow a uniform pattern. This section examines both comparisons in detail.

The percentage of Latinos, African Americans, and Whites residing in all twenty communities is shown in table 4.2. Given the unique local conditions in San Diego and Miami, the fraction of the population that is Asian and Haitian in each respective city also is included in the table. Because members of these immigrant groups tend to move initially into older areas of cities, they encounter established native-born residents who remain even after previous residents leave. In a couple of instances Latinos founded barrios or enclaves that grew into adjacent areas, and Latinos maintained that presence.

Most Latinos live in the states where these five cities are located (as well as New York), and they are increasingly concentrated in urban communities.[61] This growth is reflected in the formation of many prominent Mexican barrios. Compared with city totals, and across the rows in table 4.2, substantial percentages of Latinos do in fact reside in these barrios and enclaves. For example, Latinos dominate, or are at least more than 50 percent of the residents, in most of these communities. More than 75 percent are Latino in ten communities, and some are almost exclusively Latino—that is, approaching 90 percent or more—in every city with the exception of San Diego. According to these figures Latinos are a distinct population and reside in large and primarily intraethnic communities.

However, Latinos also reside with non-Latinos. African Americans have a large presence (more than 20 percent) in Humboldt Park, Segundo Barrio, and Wynwood. Moreover, in relative terms these neighborhoods also have African-American proportions somewhat in line with the citywide totals. However, in Miami there also has been a substantial increase in the Afro-Caribbean population, reflected in the Allapattah and Wynwood communities where Haitians reside.

In contrast, non-Latino Whites are routinely neighbors in many Chicago, El Paso, Houston, and San Diego communities. The notable

TABLE 4.2
LATINO COMMUNITIES: ETHNIC GROUP COMPARISONS
BY PERCENT, 1990

City/Community	Latino	African American	White	Asian	Haitian
Chicago					
Citywide	19	39	38	4	0
Logan Square	65	6	28	0	0
Humboldt Park	43	49	6	0	0
West Town	61	9	28	0	0
Pilsen	86	6	8	0	0
El Paso					
Citywide	69	3	27	0	0
South-Central	99	0	1	0	0
Central	89	1	10	0	0
Northeast	41	8	47	0	0
Lower Valley	88	4	7	0	0
Houston					
Citywide	27	28	41	4	0
Magnolia	86	2	12	0	0
Segundo Barrio	69	21	10	0	0
Southwest	23	18	59	0	0
Northwest	36	10	54	4	0
Miami					
Citywide	62	18	12	0	7
Allapattah	69	17	6	0	4
Wynwood	56	24	9	0	11
Little Havana	91	0	9	0	0
Latin Quarter	94	1	5	0	0
San Diego					
Citywide	20	9	59	11	0
Barrio Logan	75	13	9	1	0
Downtown	37	12	44	5	0
San Ysidro	75	4	12	8	0
Otay Mesa	58	4	20	17	0

Source: U.S. Bureau of the Census, 1990.

exceptions are El Paso and Miami, where (as we will see in stronger terms in table 4.3) few Whites or Blacks live in or around the Cuban-dominated enclave of Little Havana or El Paso barrios. In addition, Asians live on the San Diego border, especially in Otay Mesa and San Ysidro, but this is a unique situation.

Nativity Concentration

Latinos have historically had more contact with foreign and native-born coethnics. According to the historian George Sanchez,[62] between 1920 and 1930 the influx of foreign-born Mexicans grew from twice as many to five times as many foreign newcomers than native-born Mexicans in the Southern California and Texas regions.[63] By 1960, however, most Latino residents were native-born or the child of at least one native-born parent, and the Latino population in Chicago, San Diego, and Houston comprised single-digit percentages of the total population. The Latino population doubled ten years later, but many Latinos still were born in their respective state of residence. Even though the exception was El Paso,[64] the fraction of San Diego's, Houston's, and Chicago's population that was Latino increased again in 1990 to about a quarter of city's residents.[65]

Much of this growth was attributed to the Mexican population, and that trend continues in contemporary society. As expected, in table 4.3 the percentage of Mexicans continues to shape the Latino population in the El Paso, Houston, and San Diego barrios. Comparisons between city and neighborhood disclose some substantial Mexican concentrations beyond the Mexican border. In Chicago's Pilsen neighborhood, much like the Hull House and South Chicago area described by Taylor in 1930, the Mexican-origin population dominates the community. Even in heavily Puerto Rican Logan Square, Humboldt Park, and West Town, many Mexicans mixed with Latinos from Central and South America.

At least in the public imagination, Cuban control over Miami and Little Havana has long been a focal point of immigration studies.[66] In the past few years observers have begun to acknowledge that not all are "exiles"; many newcomers came over during the 1980 Mariel boatlift or on boat-rafts over the past ten to fifteen years.[67] In fact, almost a third of Little Havana's residents arrived since 1980, and more than half of the adjacent Latin Quarter are new arrivals. According to these

TABLE 4.3
LATINO COMMUNITIES: LATINO AND IMMIGRANT GROUP
INDICATORS BY PERCENT, 1990

City/Community	Mexican	Puerto Rican	Cuban	Other Latino	New Immigrant
Chicago					
Citywide	13	5	1	2	8
Logan Square	26	31	2	8	13
Humboldt Park	17	24	0	2	6
West Town	32	25	0	3	13
Pilsen	81	3	0	2	22
El Paso					
Citywide	69	0	0	0	9
South-Central	99	0	0	0	23
Central	89	0	0	0	13
Northeast	41	0	0	0	4
Lower Valley	88	0	0	0	10
Houston					
Citywide	22	0	0	3	9
Magnolia	76	0	0	6	24
Segundo Barrio	67	0	0	5	13
Southwest	13	0	0	7	16
Northwest	30	0	0	0	16
Miami					
Citywide	0	3	36	20	26
Allapattah	0	6	37	26	32
Wynwood	0	22	12	22	53
Little Havana	0	2	69	20	30
Latin Quarter	0	2	46	46	52
San Diego					
Citywide	20	0	0	0	10
Barrio Logan	74	0	0	0	33
Downtown	38	0	0	0	17
San Ysidro	79	0	0	0	17
Otay Mesa	46	0	0	0	10

Source: U.S. Bureau of the Census, 1990.

figures, Cubans in the city of Miami vary by generational status even in the heart of the successful enclave.

It should also be reemphasized that Cubans do not dominate all Miami communities—other Latinos are becoming an increasingly important segment in many areas. In 1990, heavily Nicaraguan areas emerged between downtown Miami and Little Havana. Likewise, some Latino communities have a small Cuban presence, such as Wynwood, where Puerto Ricans outnumber Cubans, and even Dominicans reside in large numbers. So even though Miami has been strongly associated with the Cuban population, and still is in many areas, non-Cuban Latinos have unfortunately been largely ignored in public discourse.

Even more spectacular than the transformation in Miami from Cuban to pan-Latino was the presence of other Latinos in many areas. The number of Guatemalans[68] in Southwest Houston and in Logan Square in Chicago has skyrocketed since 1980. Some predict that other Latinos will continue to increase as communities expand and residents attempt to recruit friends and family members to toil in the new service industry.[69] All of these Latino communities have been replenished by recent immigration, and many have significant proportions of newcomers who tend to be poorer and less educated. Thus the consequences of economic status on violence should be particularly severe, but levels of crime are somewhat less than expected.

Social Class Indicators

Many late-twentieth-century social trends have worked to the disadvantage of Latino communities. According to the 1970 census, most Latinos were native-born and should be reaping the benefits of citizenship and stability. Yet few Latinos were in professional occupations, most were not graduating from high school, and many were working in the secondary sector. In fact, most males were employed as laborers, food and cleaning service workers, or in the manufacturing or construction industry, and only a few were clerical workers. While many flourished relative to conditions in their homelands, children of immigrants were isolated from Anglos and rarely interacted with people outside the barrio.[70]

The consequences of this isolation are still apparent in contemporary society.[71] A look at El Paso barrios is instructive with respect to Latino difficulty in socioeconomic indicators. In Chihuahuita (El Segundo), most of the residents were extremely poor (71 percent) in 1990 and the Latino communities of Segundo Barrio, Latin Quarter, and Barrio Logan have substantial swaths of poverty—at least 40 percent or more. Furthermore, most barrios and enclaves have levels of education (not shown here) that are the lowest in urban America, and most residents lack basic educational attainment, including a high school diploma.

A comparison to citywide levels demonstrates that lack of citizenship has not proven kind in terms of education or income. Almost without exception, Latino residents fare poorly in comparison to the rest of the city in terms of poverty and education. Given the decaying economic context, it is not surprising that Betancur[72] describes Pilsen as having "[n]egligible levels of Latino homeownership, overcrowding, arson, neglect, and high rents." The ingredients for high violent crime rates exist, and researchers should not be surprised if crime is extremely high in these areas.

Incidentally, three communities[73] were chosen as possible middle-class exceptions, preventing an all-encompassing picture of devastation. Even in these unusual instances the situation can be less than ideal, as the predominantly White Northwest Houston community has levels of poverty and education in line with the city total. Southwest Houston and Northeast El Paso fare slightly better in terms of poverty and education. But their socioeconomic conditions are not a considerable improvement over the city average.

Geographic Landscape

There is also geographic evidence confirming that Latinos usually were segregated near the downtown fringes, to a large extent isolated from mainstream, everyday life. Across the board, barrios became settlements for immigrant Mexicans, Puerto Ricans, Cubans, and later Central Americans. As soon as they arrived, immigrant Latinos were socialized and became Americanized in the barrio or enclave. Some remained near the downtown sectors of every city, creating centers for the old community and eventually tempering the importance of downtown areas as a work focus shifted to one of cultural development.[74]

Again, Miami remains a unique case for several reasons. First, as we have mentioned, the settlement pattern ensured that the Latino population spread across the city and into every neighborhood. Second, pan-Latino communities arose, such as heavily Puerto Rican Wynwood and Allapattah, both of which also contained Nicaraguans, Cubans, Dominicans, and Hondurans.[75] These neighborhoods share common immigrant experiences and problems similar to those of Mexicans and Puerto Ricans in Chicago.[76]

Originally a White enclave, Allapattah used to be a city unto itself until it was incorporated by the city of Miami in 1925.[77] The streets of Allapattah now resemble those of other immigrant Latino communities. Storefront businesses and sidewalks are dominated by Spanish-speakers listening to *merengue* or *salsa,* watching baseball, discussing politics in the home country, or drinking *café con leche* or *cerveza* at the local *bodega,* with the smell of *platanos* and *arroz con pollo* in the air. The sidewalk scene is reminiscent of a Spanish-speaking Caribbean or Central American country, and it is easy to forget that the much older African-American communities of Liberty City and Overtown are adjacent neighborhoods.

The streets in the border barrios of El Paso and San Diego resemble other poor Latino communities in many ways. Businesses serve residents who speak both English and Spanish, but the ambience is shaped by competing sounds of *Tejano* or *Norteno* music blaring from trucks amid Chicano rappers in lowriders. The air-conditioned *cantina* around the corner serves as an extended living room, and some discuss homeland politics or the latest local politico's antics, which itself is a popular form of local entertainment. Many discuss the merits of the latest boxing match between native and foreign-born Mexicans, sometimes dwelling on the merits of nativity (Who is more Mexican?) and arguing that that corresponds to who has the biggest heart and best left hook. In El Paso the Rio Grande looms on the horizon, and while life is tough in the barrio, making a living is rougher *En el Otro Lado*—the other side—which is the view from the barrio's backyard.

Almost every Latino neighborhood fits the profile of Shaw and McKay's[78] study of Chicago's troubled areas in the early 1900s and to a lesser extent Escobar's[79] World War II–era *pachuco* Los Angeles community—that is, immigrants and/or Latinos dominate, and the areas are far from trouble-free. This is an important difference, since in these earlier time periods, even in the face of consistent population turnover, many residents used to be exclusively Mexican, and to a large extent still are; but numerous Latinos are now Puerto Rican, Honduran, Nicaraguan, Dominican, and even Guatemalan, contributing to the vibrant but poor community.[80] In the final analysis, however, Latino communities are still viewed as ridden by many social problems that in turn contribute to drug-related violence and gang warfare. In the chapter that follows, the impact of these conditions will be considered in some detail for types of homicide.

5. THE ROOTS OF HOMICIDE IN THE BARRIO AND ENCLAVE

LIKE THAT OF MANY other Mariel Cubans, Hector Nuñez's[1] path to Miami was fortuitous. Claiming to be a political prisoner, he left Cuba and arrived on one of the first waves out of the Mariel port in April 1980. Similar to many other young men who crossed into the Florida Keys on overloaded boats, there was little evidence of previous problems—criminal or otherwise. His local family ties were strong; he was quickly processed by the INS and immediately released to a sister who had left Cuba in the early 1970s and who had a stable work history in the Miami area. Everything fell into place right away. Finding work quickly at a local restaurant in Little Havana, Hector was soon able to move out of his sister's house into his own modest apartment, which he shared with a couple of roommates. All seemed to be going well for Hector, whose immigrant story, like those of others before him, began as one of humble beginnings.

Within a short time, however, Hector grew restless and was attracted to Miami's nightlife. According to his sister, he stayed out late at night and drank frequently with friends, some he knew in Cuba as a child and others he met in the INS processing center. Soon he fell behind on rent and was back in her spare bedroom. To add insult to injury, he missed too much work and was fired. To forget his troubles, he went to the local pool hall around the corner, spent what little money he had from working at a variety of odd jobs in the neighborhood, played dominos, gambled on jai alai games, and drank beer with his friends. One night, after winning a pool game, an acquaintance, Javier Rodriguez, argued with another customer, Daniel Gonzalez, about the size of the bet: Was it one or two beers? The debate quickly became heated, insults were exchanged, and the two pool players pushed each other after throwing many punches and missing all of them. Javier, however, reached over to the pool rack, grabbed one, and hit Daniel over the head with a cue stick. Daniel fell to the ground, and as he rose, pulled out a handgun hidden in his sock. Hector had already risen to break up the fight. Standing where Javier had been just moments before, he was shot in the chest and immediately bled to death. The three main participants had been in Miami three months. This incident and others like it soon became part of the widely publicized Mariel crime wave.

Hector's case initially was typical of the vast majority of Mariel Cubans who found themselves in Miami. All started a new life in a new environment, most with family connections, and tried to break from their past. Unfortunately, his demise exemplified many of the homicides in the Cuban enclave of Little Havana and other Latino communities. Data taken from homicide records and discussed later in this chapter,[2] indicate that arguments primarily among fellow ethnic group members, and escalating into homicide, comprise the plurality of homicide circumstances in Miami. In fact, the largest fraction of homicides in all twenty communities across the five cities is typically connected to escalation killings. Thus Hector's encounter is not unique, but illustrates the routine nature of arguments that escalate from a nonlethal event into lethality, demonstrating the mundane origin of most homicides. This story and others like it do not illustrate distinctiveness, but the routine and relatively low rates of Latino homicide given high poverty do.

This chapter deals with specific features of Latino homicides and homicide circumstances in the various communities considered. Clearly, the existence of poverty and other neighborhood problems has long been cited as one of the most severe differences between ethnic minority and White communities in U.S. cities.[3] By drawing from cities where the Latino community's level of homicide is at or higher than the city total, I will be able to examine Latino differences relative to city averages and place cases such as the shooting death of Hector Nuñez in a broader context. Full appreciation of the circumstances faced by Latinos, and their contrasts to larger local conditions, confirms that the Latino experience, whether it is poverty, acculturation, assimilation, or even specific types of crime, cannot simply be inferred from the experiences of earlier European immigrants and other ethnic minority groups.[4]

To illustrate this point and to complete the story of Latino communities and homicide requires evidence of neighborhood crime. I described the Latino communities, including spatial patterns, in previous chapters, and now analyze their relevant crime features. These data required direct access to official police data and requisite census tract information. This chapter also benefits from my knowledge of Latinos in Miami, from formal and informal observations at cultural events in many neighborhoods and around some city agencies over the past few years, and from several hundred hours spent with the Miami Police Department Homicide Investigations Unit. I personally observed investigators "working" over two dozen homicide cases from start to finish, involving numerous interviews of witnesses and suspects, while researching hundreds of homicide reports archived in the Miami Police Department. I also draw from conversations and visits with homicide detectives in the San Diego and El Paso Police Departments, other persons in both of these Mexican-border cities, and time spent in specific "hot spots" or areas of concentrated violence on the border.

The problem posed is simple: If Latinos are crime-prone, shouldn't Latino communities be high-crime areas, at least relative to overall city rates or proportions? If the question is simple, the answer is not, for in exploring the homicide positions of these cities and communities, a wide variety of homicide types must be considered. First it will become apparent that most Latino communities are not necessarily in high-crime cities. That does not mean that Latinos are not exposed to violence—in a couple of communities gang and drug homicides reign, but even those cases are rarely a reflection of the majority of violent activities in those areas. Rather, as far as possible, the available findings point to the reminder that Latinos are long-standing U.S. citizens *and* newly established immigrants, a fact that, along with other factors, influences Latino homicide in a manner that few other ethnic groups experience. In other words, widely held interpretations of socioeconomic differences are relevant to Latinos, but so are local conditions and the position of Latinos within these cities, both historically and in contemporary settings.

UNIQUE VIOLENCE CONDITIONS

The problems associated with urban living should prove serious obstacles to Latino everyday life. Normally, the factors linked to violence are heightened in the barrio and enclave, and as a consequence Latino communities have been widely viewed as crime-prone. Historically, as we saw in chapters 2 and 3, police and teachers in El Paso singled out young barrio residents as crime-prone more than eighty years ago. In turn, some of the immigrants' children rebelled against notions of compliance, integration into mainstream Anglo society, or movement into traditional Mexican culture. Instead, a "*pachuco* gang" subculture arose, and pachucos first appeared in El Paso in the late 1920s and early 1930s.[5] These youths, dressed in distinctive "zoot suits," with long jackets, exaggerated shoulders, and hanging gold chains, emerged in the impoverished Mexican barrios of Chihuahuita or El Segundo, in the South-Central section of El Paso. The "zoot suit" phenomenon eventually spread to other barrios in the Southwest and was emulated by urban African-American and Filipino youths.[6] This figure proved critical to the shift in the public image of the "lazy" Mexican to the "violent" one, and perpetuated media stereotypes then and now.[7]

In fact, pachucos soon became targets of both law-enforcement officials and the popular media. Perhaps the most extreme example occurred in Southern California during World War II, when newspaper headlines perpetuated existing racist stereotypes of pachuco gang members as a consequence of a "primitive and backward culture endemic in the Mexican colonias" growing through Southern California.[8] Within this vein of stereotypes, the Los Angeles County Sheriff's Department produced a report, written by Lt. Ed Duran Ayres, claiming that Mexicans were naturally disposed to violence, with biological urges to "to kill, or at least let blood." Supposedly this desire, at least according to the Ayres Report, was traced to an utter disregard for the value of life among the Aztec population, having threatening consequences and potentially destroying the fabric of American life.

The contemporary homicide link to the past is not always explicit or apparent in routine statistics. As seen in the previous chapter, the birthplace of the pachuco is in a barrio, with one of the most disadvantaged urban conditions among *any* neighborhood. Not only has the past affected current sentiments, but contemporary public policies also have a bearing on their development. The Border Patrol has long block-aded the international border, straddling the barrio, in an attempt to keep out the "hordes" of immigrants ostensibly waiting to wreak havoc in America.[9] Latinos are still widely viewed as a danger to contemporary society, committing crimes, abusing social programs, and changing America in an alarming manner.[10] Yet if these notions are correct, El Paso's barrios should have alarming levels of crime.[11] In fact, no other Latino community in this set of twenty has a higher level of economic decay than the El Paso barrios.

If crime and criminal involvement parallel poverty, the presence of homicides in Latino communities should appear more so than in other areas, especially in the heavily impoverished Latino barrios. As we see in table 5.1, that association appears, but the extent is not as severe as anticipated based on theory and research. When extreme poverty and extremely low educational attainment converge in violent crime ac-counts, astronomical homicide rates should be expected in such areas. There were five barrios (four in San Diego and one in El Paso) at least twice as high as the respective city rate, and one Chicago community (Humboldt Park) came close to that relative measure. The reminder in table 5.1 that San Diego already has a much lower homicide rate (.121 per 1,000) than those in similarly sized cities (.319 per 1,000), how-ever, tempers this finding of high-crime barrios.

For perspective, consider Barrio Logan, the highest-rate community in this table and with a poverty rate 3.4 times higher than the local rate. The San Diego barrio reported an average homicide rate of .645 per 1,000 residents, or 64.5 per 100,000 residents. Although 5.3 times higher than the city average, this level surpasses the national homicide rate (31.9) for cities with more than 1 million residents by a ratio of just over two to one.

Another barrio that emerged with homicide rates almost three times higher than the local average is South-Central El Paso. Although high, yet again, this rate needs to be treated with caution. To begin with, recall that the citywide rate (.067) is already extremely low and one of the lowest in the country of cities with more than 500,000 pop-ulation. In addition, during this time the barrio average is still among the lowest in all Latino communities in this study.

The most interesting difference is not within cities but with other Latino communities; the most obvious example is the similarity between

TABLE 5.1
LATINO COMMUNITIES: HOMICIDE RATES PER 1,000 RESIDENTS

City and Type	Homicide Rate	City and Type	Homicide Rate
Major City	.319	**Large-Size City**	.246
(million-plus persons)		*(500,000 to 999,999 persons)*	
Chicago		*El Paso*	
Citywide	.281	Citywide	.067
Logan Square	.216	South-Central	.180
Humboldt Park	.533	Central	.078
West Town	.282	Northeast	.058
Pilsen	.323	Lower Valley	.115
Houston			
Citywide	.318	**Medium-Size City**	.217
Magnolia	.345	*(250,000 to 499,999 persons)*	
Segundo Barrio	.541	*Miami*	
Southwest	.206	Citywide	.378
Northwest	.205	Allapattah	.226
San Diego		Wynwood	.265
Citywide	.121	Little Havana	.189
Barrio Logan	.645	Latin Quarter	.269
Downtown	.456		
San Ysidro	.270		
Otay Mesa	.596		

Sources: Population estimates based on data from the U.S. Bureau of the census. Homicide data are from respective police departments. National data from Fox and Zawitz, 1999.

Note: Annual average over 1985–95.

the El Paso barrio and Little Havana. Both have identical homicide rates and are overwhelmingly Latino in terms of both city and community presence. But, surprisingly, killings in the birthplace of the pachuco are equivalent to those in the home of the "Golden Exiles," even though each has a vastly different history of settlement, accommodation, and economic conditions. This is not to say that violent activity is nonexistent in the barrio or pervasive in the exile community, but if violence is indeed a reflection of serious problems in the barrio or stability in the enclave, the reality is that those expected levels are not reflected in this table.

HOMICIDE CIRCUMSTANCES UP CLOSE

There are a number of basic forces that have led to arguments turning lethal, and I viewed their consequences up close in Miami. For analytic purposes it might be useful to distinguish among these cases, but they make sense when viewed *in toto* as a picture with numerous pieces. One strand involved a combination of elements. I turn to a homicide scene (whose investigation I personally followed) in Miami in about 1997. The body of the victim, a Salvadoran male in his midtwenties, lay on the sidewalk in front of a *bodega*. Several potential witnesses hovered inside the bar but none was willing to provide an account to the detectives since they all claimed to be in the bathroom at the time of the shooting. Despite the lack of witness cooperation, after a couple of days the homicide detectives were able to locate the shooter, a Puerto Rican male in his late thirties who resided fifteen minutes away from the crime scene. The suspect initially denied any involvement, claiming he was with his wife the night of the shooting. After the detectives confronted him with some evidence—an eyewitness in another bar across from the crime scene saw him leave the scene on his bicycle—and his wife stating on a speakerphone that she was not at home the night of the shooting, the offender wilted and confessed to the killing. According to his confession, the victim and offender were drinking acquaintances. They spent the day watching a soccer game on *Galavision* in the lounge along with several bar patrons. After several hours and several beers together an argument broke out between the two. The shooter accidentally brushed the victim's backside as he stood up to use the bathroom. Despite some familiarity with each other, the victim apparently misinterpreted the gesture and proceeded to verbally humiliate the offender and challenged his manhood in front of the other bar patrons. The shooter, recognizing that the victim was younger and stronger, told everyone in the bar that he would not forget the insult. He arose, got on his bike, went home, retrieved his handgun, and rode his bike back to the *bodega*. The victim, in spite of warnings from the patrons that the shooter would return, decided to drink another beer and went outside to smoke a cigarette. As he finished his smoke, the offender returned, parked his bike, and began to shoot at the soon-to-be victim. The victim started to turn away from the shooter and into the doorway, making it back into the entry, but was hit twice and fell to the ground. His assailant announced: "I finish what I start" and pointed his gun at each onlooker, asking them if they saw anything. All of them answered "No," and he left the crime scene.[12] After the detectives asked him why he shot the victim, the shooter claimed (in Spanish) that "he touched my ass not once but twice; wouldn't you do the same thing?" The detectives replied they now understood his actions and arrested him.

The most important point in these routine killings, involved here, in one way or another, are the following factors: victim-precipitated arguments between acquaintances; fights over pool games or some other sporting event; brawls involving female companionship or the lack of it; and altercations in bars or retaliations over earlier alcohol-induced fights. These features differ little from the kinds of things that lead to homicide among other ethnic groups. In fact, these events are also common across all Latino groups and are not ethnic or group-specific motivations. As Martinez, Lee, and Nielsen[13] observe in a recent study of Miami, because immigrant Latinos were never unusually violent, despite dominant themes in popular stereotypes, their crime-prone legacy is more myth than reality.

To a certain degree, escalation homicides involve different interactions than those between strangers. After all, robberies are routine violent acts. There is no rigorous study I know of that examines Latino robbery homicide, but the evidence I have pieced together from hundreds of supplemental reports and observations seems to indicate that while persistent in poor urban neighborhoods, most characteristics are similar to other types of homicide, with, of course, its chief distinction—stealing something of value. This personal observation at a crime scene provides typical details: Four young Spanish-speaking males in the middle of the day robbed the *bodega*. All wore masks, were armed with handguns, and knew exactly where the entrances and exists were throughout the store. In the span of a few minutes, one stood guard by the front, another emptied the cash registers, while a third searched customers' and store employees' pockets. The fourth escorted the owner—a recent arrival from the Dominican Republic via New York City—to the office safe in the back of the store. As the robbers looted the cash drawers and prodded the shoppers into a corner, the contents of the safe were emptied into a garbage bag. The robbers moved toward the entrance but, as an apparent warning to all, the last one turned and shot an employee, the butcher, who was standing in the back. At that point everyone hit the floor and did not look up for several minutes. The elements of planning, surprise, and disguise distinguish some routine robberies from other violent crimes. Add the stranger component and it is apparent why no one was ever arrested for this homicide.

As noted earlier, killings between intimates could assume many characteristics inherent in other homicides. But still they vary in at least two important respects—they are typically male on female, and the victim and offender are (or were) in an intimate, usually sexual, relationship. Despite these distinctions, there is nothing comparable to the level of escalation homicides. On the other hand, intimate killings can assume certain elements seen in escalation or robbery homicides. Lovers argue over money, drug or alcohol use, previous relationships, even attention paid to others outside the current relationship, or a host of other elements. The consequences also can differ in one way from other homicides. That is apparent in the case of murder/suicides. I draw this time from an experience in Little Havana: The killer had seriously assaulted his wife at least once before the fatal shooting. He hit her two years before for serving a male guest first in "his" household during dinner. After that, he hit the guest several times for taking the food *before* the head of the household. Both victims suffered head lacerations and required medical attention, but their wounds were not fatal. At that point the violator left the apartment and sought refuge in the neighborhood. But it took longer than usual to locate and arrest him. Apparently he was a "local" war hero, having served with distinction in the Cuban Army during the Angolan Civil War. Many neighbors held him in high regard and put him up for several nights, although it was not clear if they were completely aware of his predicament. Other locals were aware of his circumstances or at least were not swayed by his exploits in the old country. A local female resident, who actually went out on the streets for several nights directing domestic violence detectives to his rumored hideouts, eventually discovered his hideout and turned him in. After serving a short sentence, the assaulter reconciled with his wife. Daily life resumed, and the police were never called back to the residence. Nevertheless, one night, the neighbors heard several screams and shouts. They also heard three gunshots. As the police arrived, and as the detectives entered the scene, one of them noted: "It looks like a murder/suicide to me," a particular type of intimate homicide—one where the male intimate shoots and kills his female partner and then himself.""

In short, these cases are tragic and equally serious when compared to each other. But it is important to remember that while homicide circumstances vary in these qualitative descriptions, the quantitative data presented in this book demonstrate that Latinos *themselves* are not overly involved in these situations. These observations were provided to describe the routine interaction between acquaintances and intimates described in these accounts as well as the serious robbery encounter observed earlier. They offer a stark contrast to the sensationalistic imagery of high-rate killers or drug/gang lords reported in the media.

Most homicides involved a combination of elements—alcohol involvement, imagined or real slights, and available weapons, especially guns, that escalated into arguments that turned lethal. Robbery was a partial exception, but even in that instance, the homicide appeared unexceptional. The end result of these homicides was not a function of the unique characteristics or culture of Latinos but factors that have historically shaped the violence of all ethnic groups in this country.[14] While the factors shaping Latino homicide, such as immigration, presumably are different, the circumstances surrounding the Latino homicide experience in and of itself exhibit characteristics that influence many homicides regardless of ethnicity. In contrast, recall that earlier in this book, William I. Thomas and Florian Znaniecki[15] argued that Polish immigrants were more likely to kill strangers in the United States than in Poland because of disorganization, while the stories in this section point to acquaintance homicides, as do a couple of Mariel homicide papers mentioned in the literature review. Perhaps the statistical data better demonstrate this than stories illustrating ordinary circumstances.

Homicide Motivations

There is no doubt that substandard education and poor economic conditions breed violent crime such as homicide, and certain types of homicide in particular. Pundits have been especially concerned with the prevalence of drug, gang, and intimate homicides among the immigrant (Latino) population.[16] Although Latinos comprised a small part of the nation's population, they regularly constituted the stereotype of drug trafficking crime in recent movies such as *Scarface, Colors, Ameri-*

can Me, Carlito's Way, and *Traffic*, which contribute to the perception that drugs and gangs rule Latino communities.[17] Diego Castro, in his essay "Media: 'Hot Blood and Easy Virtue': Mass Media and the Making of Racist Latino/a Stereotypes," describes how "From the 1970s through the 1990s, gang films continued to proliferate, becoming more and more explicit in their depictions of Latinos as drug-dealing, gun-toting, menacing characters who daily commit unimaginable criminal acts, mostly against innocent whites."[18]

Along these lines, in yet another essay in the same volume as Castro's, Alberto Mata notes how politicians use these images to promote fear of Latinos, since they "promote homogenous images of Latinos as drug lords aiming to destroy America's youths through drugs, as dangerous gang bangers who shoot anyone unfortunate enough to stumble through their neighborhoods, or as poor peasants crossing the border to have babies in U.S. hospitals so that their children will become American citizens and thus inappropriately be eligible for a broad range of entitlements. These suspect images of Latinos/as as criminal, vicious, and sneaky are very powerful and mute calmer voices claiming otherwise." These examples are not centered on fact but myth. During the 1985 to 1995 period, for example, drug- and gang-related homicides peaked across the United States, but Latinos, as we shall see, were rarely overinvolved in this activity.

While other places may have large immigrant Latino communities and urban crime problems, few have been labeled as crime-prone and singled out for public debate as much as in the communities in these five cities. This media treatment occurred in the midst of the 1980 Mariel boatwave, especially in Miami, and arose again in the early 1990s, but immigrant Latinos were concentrated only in a handful of places outside of South Florida and Southern California. There, immigrant Latinos was targeted as dangerous criminals with the same media frenzy as pachucos in an earlier generation and Mariels in Miami ten years earlier. The origins of this stereotype are old, and the immigrant hysteria continues today much as in the past. In short, as with the evidence presented in chapter 4, little proof exists that at the neighborhood level crime is high or Latinos are violence-prone, in particular with regard to drugs and gangs.

Nevertheless, table 5.2 indicates just how widely local violence was largely shaped by events unique to each city and in some situations

TABLE 5.2
LOCAL CONDITIONS AND VIOLENCE CONCENTRATIONS

	Drug Cartel/ Trafficking	Heightened Gang Activity	Unique Events
Chicago	No	Yes	Industrial decline
El Paso	Yes	No	"Hold the line"
Houston	Yes	No	Oil bust
Miami	Yes	No	Mariels
San Diego	Yes	Yes	Gang/border crossings

Sources: Sanders 1994; Gonzalez 2000; Inciardi 1992; Martinez 1994; Nevins, 2002; Padilla 1993; Rodriguez 1993.

influenced Latino areas. Certainly Latinos living in the Sunbelt cities were probably exposed to violence between drug cartels and over drug trafficking in most Latino neighborhoods. These cities are conduits to the rest of the country, and it stands to reason that all types of commerce (legal and illegal) spread out from the border, which also is home to a large transient population that crosses the border and moves north. Though there was a significant concentration level of heightened gang activity in the Chicago Puerto Rican and San Diego Mexican barrios, others were not exposed to street gang violence. By and large, however, the violence concentrations were shaped by events unique to each city and in some cases directly influenced Latino communities, as in the case of INS operations on the two border cities and the Mariel influx in Miami. On the one hand, the data in these tables dispel the myth of the unusually violent killer, also illustrated in the homicide stories, while on the other they maintain the argument that Latino experience is different from that of previous groups since Latinos have lower levels of homicide than expected despite exposure to these local and unique drug/gang/immigrant conditions. The absence, not the presence, of drug- and gang-related killings is the story in these tables.

Still, some communities did suffer from the ravages of violence accompanying the drug trade, as seen in table 5.3. Barrio Logan had a well-known reputation as the center of gang activity in San Diego, much like the barrios in Los Angeles that had an old street gang tradition.[19] Since at least the 1970s *La Eme* has had a presence, and members of the *Calle 30* or *Logans 30s* worked on both sides of the U.S.-Mexico border.[20] Collecting data for his book *Gangbangs and Drive-bys* William B.

TABLE 5.3

LATINO COMMUNITIES: TYPES OF HOMICIDE MOTIVES
BY PERCENT, 1990

City/Community	Drug	Intimate	Escalation	Robbery	Gang	Felony
Chicago						
Citywide	13	8	41	10	16	11
Logan Square	9	7	35	9	30	10
Humboldt Park	23	5	28	10	12	12
West Town	5	3	34	8	26	8
Pilsen	4	3	32	8	41	12
El Paso						
Citywide	2	19	28	6	14	2
South Central	6	11	33	22	22	6
Central	4	12	58	7	12	5
Northeast	4	28	44	12	8	4
Lower Valley	3	6	31	9	18	6
Houston						
Citywide	18	14	39	18	2	9
Magnolia	10	13	51	12	6	8
Segundo Barrio	7	4	61	14	0	13
Southwest	19	15	36	15	2	14
Northwest	5	16	39	18	5	15
Miami						
Citywide	16	11	36	20	1	6
Allapattah	16	16	31	13	0	15
Wynwood	4	0	41	32	0	14
Little Havana	5	31	39	21	0	0
Latin Quarter	11	15	41	15	0	9
San Diego						
Citywide	20	23	20	14	18	3
Barrio Logan	37	10	23	4	24	2
Downtown	30	9	26	13	22	1
San Ysidro	3	19	8	38	5	0
Otay Mesa	1	22	33	44	0	0

Sources: Homicide data from respective police departments

Sanders[21] noted how "These were Mexican-American gangs living in the working- and lower-class barrios, especially those in the South Bay area near the Mexican border." While originated as fighting gangs, a transformation occurred as the lucrative crack and crank trade generated illegal activity both in and out of the barrio, and the complexities of violence and immigration can again be explored at the community level.

The most obvious pattern is that 37 percent of Barrio Logan's homicides in table 5.3 were directly related to drugs, the highest fraction of drug-related homicides[22] in any of the twenty communities. However, these were not in open-air drug markets, but indoors, where dealers and customers were targets of home invasions. Some killings occurred while dealers were intercepted during a delivery, others happened when drugs were in a residence and a "crew" was sent in to retrieve them, and a few more were over drug turf or deals gone awry.[23]

Many, however, arose over mundane matters. The SDPD reports homicides that started over the *quality* of dope.[24] Arguments and assaults preceded some of these killings in a manner similar to the escalation killings noted earlier in this chapter. Gang members approach adversaries, as the case of "Jésus Espinoza," a reputed member of *3000 Logan* accosting "José Morales," an associate of the *Diablos,* both San Diego street gangs. As Morales left a neighborhood bar on Imperial Street, Espinoza, who had been waiting in the parking lot of this known Diablos hangout, asked him where he was "from" and who he "represented." Morales replied "Diablos rule" and threw a beer bottle at him. Espinoza pulled out a gun and said, "Your Carnales sold me some bunk mota" and shot at him. Although not fatally wounded, Morales crawled back toward the bar, and Espinoza shot a second time, this time hitting him in the chest area. An SDPD patrol car—which had been called to the adjacent liquor store for a shoplifting case—arrived at the moment Espinoza tried to flee the scene, and the officers immediately apprehended him.

At times, however, the realities of life in the barrio proved harsher than a simple drug or nondrug homicide. Rather, competition over the drug trade in the 1980s was probably an extension of violence that predated the growth of crack or any other drug. Tensions had long been high in Barrio Logan (and in Chicago barrios) and had been exacerbated through multiple generations of gang life, which in turn generated gang activity, retaliations, and homicide over turf and petty slights. Barrio gangs were involved in large portions of barrio homicides, but this finding is, again, diminished by the reminder that the San Diego homicide rate was not substantially higher than for other cities with more than a million residents.[25]

The drug and gang pattern documented in San Diego was not readily evident in other Latino communities, with the partial exception of Chicago. Table 5.3 shows that none of these communities reached the dominating levels of drug-related homicide seen in other cities,[26] but some did attain fractions of gang-related homicides exceeding the city average. Latino ethnicity aside, *all* of the Latino Chicago communities exceeded the total city percent of homicides linked to gangs and gang members.[27]

In these cases, territory was encroached, honor was important, and retaliations were perceived as necessary, so killings continued. That was evident especially in Pilsen and, to a lesser, but still substantial degree, in Logan Square, West Town, and Humboldt Park, where gang-related killings provided a second major pattern. Much of this violence was between warring gang members fighting over a previous transgression; *barrio* control and turf; lingering insults, imagined or otherwise; and honor, in some circumstances emerging out of verbal disputes that turned lethal. A few, of course, were random drive-by shootings where a street target or house was chosen, and a bystander was shot—some innocent, some not. The implication is that this process has nothing to do with ethnicity per se but rather mirrors the local milieu.

Ironically, media-created events might have exacerbated some gang homicides. In his autobiography *My Bloody Life: The Making of a Latin King*, ex-gang member Reymundo Sanchez[28] describes one Chicago summer, and how a youth crime wave was perpetuated: "The local news station began reporting on the savagery of Latino youth. Gang colors, hand signs, and graffiti were all covered on television. Most of the information reported was inconsistent or fabricated. Gangbangers avoided reporters and their camera like the plague. Reporters didn't care. They would talk to any kid who was willing to be on television. The result was that kids ignorant of the ways of the gangs told stories they had heard as if they had firsthand experience. These kids ended up as targets for gang members at school as well as in their own neighborhoods. Without realizing it the news media had endangered the lives of these kids. . . . The innocent kids who didn't know enough not to talk to reporters became the victims of gang media hype. Kids who otherwise shied away from gang activity were not looking to join a gang for protection."

Again, although not a definitive explanation of the rise of gang homicides in Chicago, this example does provide further illustration of the role the media create in perpetuating the image of the crime-prone Latino youth and by extension the violent Latino gang member.

Across the main categories of homicide, a third type regularly dominates and routinely cuts across all types of homicides and communities. Interpersonal conflicts, involving arguments over perceived disrespect, male fights over female attention, and displays of machismo are all regularly exacerbated in an atmosphere of heightened tension that can escalate into killings. The street corners, cheap housing, bars and nightclubs that attract drug dealers and gang members also contribute to a milieu where nonlethal disputes turn lethal.[29] A look, giving someone the eye, or even an accidental brush requires some type of response, and at times this is violent. Having been reduced to a physical response to a verbal challenge, or vice versa, a victim or an offender loses prestige if no defense of honor is advanced, and the episode often escalates into a lethal event.

An observer would note that this typology also appeared in other downtown San Diego neighborhoods and was *not* exclusive to the barrio. Instead, the Yuppie area adjacent to the barrio and in the heart of downtown displayed the same drug and gang contour despite having far fewer Latinos, less poverty, and more educated residents than Barrio Logan.[30] About a third of homicides were drug-related, and gang-motivated killings comprised a fifth to a quarter of all killings in both center city neighborhoods.

Drug, gang, and escalation killings reigned near the central business district, just as in the barrio or in any other city. This is important to note, since it would be inaccurate to label Latinos as more prone to these types of homicide when others nearby are engaging in the same activity, at least in similar proportions. Rather, the dope and gangbanging milieu sweeping urban American hit the heart of some Latino communities like any other neighborhood, but the impact was relatively less in San Diego and rarely comprised the majority of all homicides.

The drug/gang epidemic did not hit the border hard. On the far south side of San Diego are San Ysidro and Otay Mesa. The street life in these neighborhoods, while bearing many similarities to that in Barrio Logan, is organized around movement into and out of the Mexican border. Groups of young men and women can be seen getting off and onto the trolley leaving people at the last train stop, and crossing into Mexico. There is a rush of excitement as both residents and nonresidents push through the point of entry. Others come to and go from Tijuana into San Diego, many take the train to school or work downtown, but others stay in the border neighborhoods.

Working in the neighborhoods described above are noncitizens with worker permits, student visas, or other official documents providing temporary entry into the San Diego area. For a variety of reasons, many of those of Mexican origin possess the paperwork allowing routine movement into San Diego. Those without documentation are forced to enter by other means and become inviting targets for robbers (on both sides of the border) who are waiting for them to cross near the San Ysidro entry or through the numerous canyons dotting Otay Mesa and the surrounding area.

The two border communities differ sharply from the barrio in levels of homicide and motivation. Recall table 5.1, which shows that homicide rates in San Ysidro are substantially lower than in center city areas, but higher than the rate for San Diego as a whole. However, the rate in Otay Mesa is almost as high as in the barrio. Note that both border spots were dominated by lethal robberies, usually of "clandestine" immigrants serving as prey to bandits in the numerous adjacent and sparsely occupied canyons. Most victims are not residents but workers moving through the area and in some cases returning to serve previous employers.

Others were killed over arguments after celebrating a successful border crossing. Even though the victim and the offender were in the isolated canyons, some circumstances shaping killings that gave rise to lethality remained the same as elsewhere. A few of these arguments turned lethal after debates on *where* to migrate escalated after crossing into the many canyons. The fact that Otay Mesa's homicide rate was higher than those for contiguous San Ysidro, to a certain extent reflects the small numbers of residents in the area; the homicide rate is high due to a relatively low population base. Nevertheless, all of these findings are in a major city (San Diego) that as a whole exhibits lower than expected levels of homicide, as we saw in the first table of this chapter.

It must be reiterated that in Miami over the 1985 to 1995 period, homicide was indeed a problem within this multiethnic city, and it had been a problem for a number of years.[31] As I previously noted, drug warfare in the 1980s gave rise to the "Scarface Legacy" and "Cocaine Cowboys" stereotypes in the popular media, and an anti-immigrant hysteria developed that attempted to label Latino immigrants as responsible for the growing drug trade. It is true that drug-motivated homicides were higher in Miami than in Chicago and El Paso. The Latino communities, however, may have been outlets for drugs or served as distribution points to other parts of the country, but the level of drug killings never exceeded the local standard (even when the local standard was presumably high). Only the neighborhood of Allapattah met the overall city percentage. But even the percentage of homicides related to drugs was in a community with a lower than average homicide rate. The low drug-related fraction demonstrates the lack of validity of using Latinos and immigrant Latino communities as sources of the drug-related hysteria that proliferated during this time.

While most Latino communities were not as violent-crime-prone as expected given extreme deprivation, neither were they violence-free. Some barrios had levels of homicide higher than the city total, and drug/gang-related killings were rampant in some spots. The main finding in these communities is that these incidents never reached epidemic proportions and rarely overwhelmed[32] the diverse Latino community, at least to the extent portrayed in the media or announced by policymakers. Nevertheless, Latino communities, especially old border barrios, had plenty of social, demographic, and economic reasons to be crime-prone and supportive of violent activity given overwhelming levels of economic deprivation.

This is especially evident when measured in terms of ethnicity, immigration, poverty, and education. The quality of life in all twenty Latino communities was overwhelmingly substandard, and residents were living below the poverty line, anywhere from one-quarter in the vaunted heart of the exile community (Little Havana) to more than 70 percent in some older border barrios. The large numbers of immigrants residing in the area, who are typically impoverished, probably affected the local economic conditions. The Latino community across the country is overwhelmingly immigrant, poor, and poorly educated, and not a single cohesive group as popularly portrayed in the media.[33]

   Despite the historical demonizing of Latinos and the recent characterization of immigrants as crime-prone, little evidence exists to support these stereotypes. The historian David G. Gutierrez[34] notes that contemporary images of Mexican immigrants are linked to a wide range of social problems, including "increasing crime rates, drug abuse, and gang activity in the cities," that propel negative opinion of Latinos and immigrants, creating resistance to immigration, and fueling acts of violence against immigrants. These incidents and portrayals are not based on empirical reality or facts, but on fiction and fears. The next chapter demonstrates this, over time and in comparison with similarly situated ethnic minority groups.

6. THE ETHNIC AND IMMIGRANT HOMICIDE CONTRAST, 1980-95

IT HAS BECOME COMMONPLACE in the social science literature and popular media to note that racial differences exist, at least in terms of Black versus White distinctions, in a host of social issues such as poverty, income, fertility, family structure, voting patterns, occupation patterns, and residential segregation. Throughout most of the post–World War II period, however, James F. Short Jr., in *Poverty, Ethnicity, and Violent Crime,* contends[1] that "attention has focused on crimes committed by 'persons of color,' especially by African Americans, the vast majority of whom are native born." Nowhere has this race and crime comparison occurred more than in studies on homicide. Because a majority of ethnic minorities was Black and thus easier to single out rather than Latinos in most U.S. recordkeeping systems, it could be argued that it is important to concentrate on White versus Black time trend comparisons. Sharp differences are easier to observe when substantial data exist and evidence is available from different sources, allowing explanations of levels and changes in violence.

Still, Short[2] notes: "The ethnicity of criminals and their victims often has reflected the recency of arrival in this country of immigrants." Will this be the case for Latinos? If so, how and why? There is no doubt that racial and ethnic groups display variations in their homicide rates for a variety of reasons, including differences in the causes leading to their location of settlement in the United States, the manner in which they were received, and the community conditions they encounter daily. For these reasons it is easy to see why many would speculate that the circumstances confronting Latinos should impact violent crime, although, as we saw in the previous chapter, the impact of neighborhood-level influences was less extreme than predicted. This chapter considers these characteristics relative to Blacks and Whites throughout a period when sharp rises in violence captured the national imagination and high crime rates were often characterized as an ethnic minority group attribute.[3]

Despite the temptation to portray violent-crime differences among Whites, African Americans, and Latinos as the result of "culture," this type of explanation is not the most prominent in the literature review in chapter 1. In terms of concrete implications for each ethnic group, net of economic characteristics, culture is difficult to uniformly compare and contrast. However, the differences between the conditions under which the new immigrant Latinos arrived and the circumstances facing older Latinos in the barrios and Blacks in similar areas are subtle at best—that is, poverty and other indicators of urban decay reign in both instances, but circumstances left behind in the home country are usually much worse for foreign-born newcomers than for native-born Blacks in urban America. Contemporary urban conditions are hard to overcome, and violence is concentrated in areas where ethnic minorities reside, with few exceptions. The primary difference is that Latino violence is less widespread than thought. With that in mind, I examine ethnic-group homicide offender trends. I conclude with subgroup differences in homicide offending.

HOMICIDE OVER TIME

Scholars have noted that the leading source of homicide variation is a direct, or sometimes indirect, reflection of socioeconomic conditions.[4] Income, education, employment, housing conditions, and the like are all factors that typically influence violent crime. Consideration of the different levels of these factors experienced by Whites, Blacks, and Latinos therefore provides a useful indicator of these groups' relative positions in the United States.

Examination of homicide experiences by and against Latinos generally indicates higher rates than for the White segment of the population and lower rates than that of African Americans. However, African American homicide is for the most part far higher than the rate for Latinos.[5] Indeed, the magnitude of these differences suggests that the Latino experience is radically different from that of Blacks, notwithstanding the obvious fact that Latinos are at an economic disadvantage when compared to Whites and in line with that of Blacks.[6]

Certain data limitations should be noted before turning to the findings. First, the African American population is very small in El Paso and a relatively small ethnic group in San Diego. Undoubtedly this is linked in some manner to the large military presence in both cities, but the data do not permit separation of military from others, residents from nonresidents, or any other distinction. Second, fluctuations in the rate of African-American homicide are susceptible to small increases in the number of killings, and this is reflected in the graphs. This case holds in particular for El Paso, but there is a reasonable degree of consistency in the level of homicides of all cities studied. Finally, most of the graph lines are statistically smoothed (i.e., averaged over three years) to aid in visual display. The exceptions are in the last two figures (Mariels and Mexican border killings) since the numbers are so small that smoothing is not appropriate (see figures 6.6 and 6.7).

In most of the five cities selected for this study, Latinos had homicide offender rates persistently lower than African Americans in *nearly all* years between 1980 and 1995. In turn, Latinos *usually* had higher homicide rates than Whites. Not only does this pattern maintain itself throughout fifteen years for all of the groups, but also in most cases the gap between African Americans and Latinos is much greater than between Latinos and Whites. In a number of years the latter gap vanishes in Latino-dominated El Paso and Miami (see figures 6.1 and 6.2). Even though several waves of immigrants hit Miami hard and El Paso was the target of numerous border crossings, presumably causing local strife if not contributing indirectly to violent crime such as homicide throughout this period, Latinos were not affected in terms of turmoil and intentional violent deaths. For example, in 1995, homicide rates in the two Latino-majority cities were 4.45 and 12.3, and 5.9 and 9.4 per 100,000 for Whites and Latinos in El Paso and Miami, respectively. Similarly, the Latino/Black gap is usually three to four times greater for Blacks than for Latinos throughout this period in both predominantly

FIGURE 6.1
MIAMI HOMICIDE OFFENDER RATES: ETHNIC TRENDS AND COMPARISONS

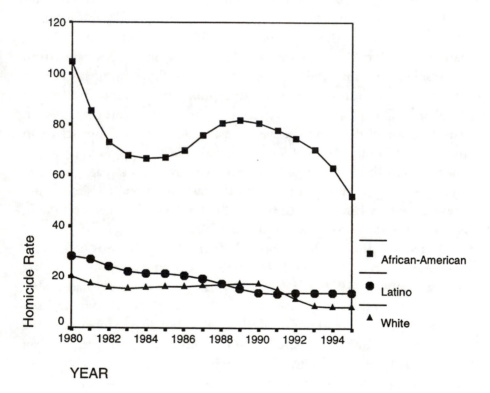

Source: Miami Police Department Homicide Investigation Unit.

FIGURE 6.2
EL PASO HOMICIDE OFFENDER RATES: ETHNIC TRENDS
AND COMPARISONS

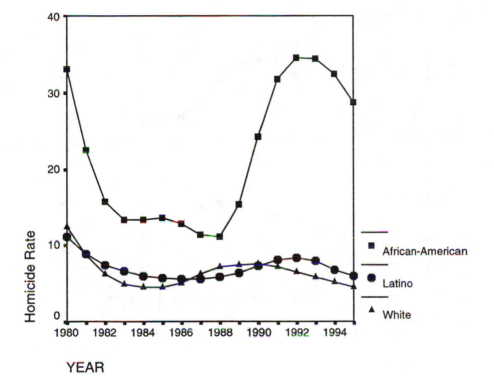

Source: El Paso Police Department Homicide Investigation Unit.

FIGURE 6.3

SAN DIEGO HOMICIDE OFFENDER RATES: ETHNIC TRENDS
AND COMPARISONS

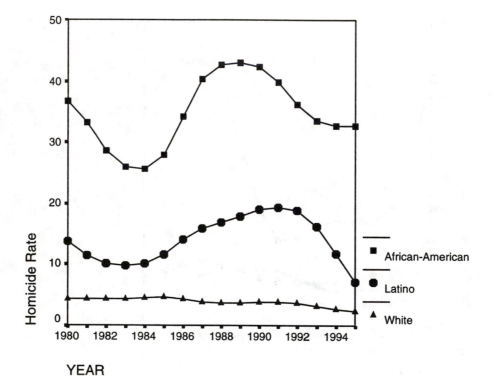

Source: San Diego Police Department Homicide Investigation Unit.

FIGURE 6.4
HOUSTON HOMICIDE OFFENDER RATES: ETHNIC TRENDS AND COMPARISONS

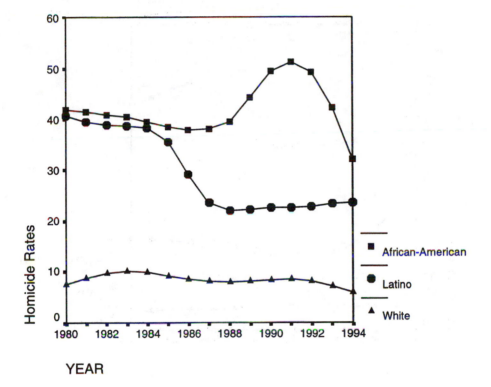

Source: City of Houston Police Department Homicide Investigation Unit.

FIGURE 6.5

CHICAGO HOMICIDE OFFENDER RATES: ETHNIC TRENDS
AND COMPARISONS

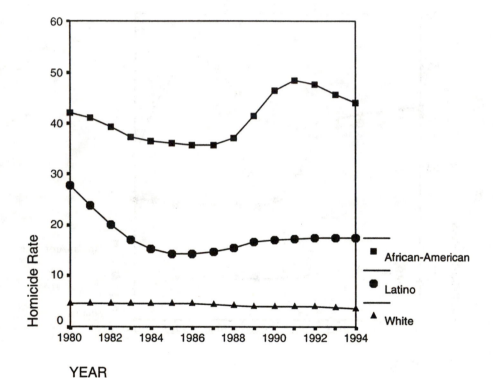

Source: Homicide in Chicago, 1965–1995.

Latino cities. All of this suggests that if immigrant Latinos were aggravating local conditions, it was not quite as badly as the situation for Blacks in these two cities. Indeed, the former clearly improved in their position relative to Whites in terms of closing the homicide gap.

Other data suggest that when Latinos are smaller fractions of the population, and in major cities with old barrios, the gap with Whites is substantially wider. Figure 6.3 provides homicide rates for the three ethnic groups for San Diego over all sixteen years. Comparisons made at five-year intervals are rather revealing. In 1980 the homicide offender rate for Latinos of 14.5 was three times that of White killers (4.7) but two and a half times less than that of Blacks (36.8). Five years later the gap narrowed as rates declined, but the magnitude rose again in 1990. The Latino (Mexican) homicide rate was almost six times greater than the White rate and two times lower than the Black rate. The gap in 1995 should have held to the 1990 rates, but instead the White/Latino gap closed and the Latino/Black disparity widened.

The pattern is somewhat different in Chicago (see figure 6.5). At least initially, the White-to-Latino gap was greater than on the border. Chicago's factories faltered, work became scarce, and the decade started out rough for Latinos. In 1980 the Latino homicide rate was six times that of Whites; five years later the magnitude dropped to three times but later grew back up, to five times that of Whites. By contrast, the 1980 Latino homicide rate started one and a half times less than that of Blacks but widened and remained about two and a half times lower throughout the remainder of the 1980s and to 1994.

With one notable exception in figure 6.4, the Latino killing rate fell between Blacks and Whites in Houston. The "oil bust" of the early 1980s was that exception, as the Latino and African-American rates remained the same until 1985, and Latino homicide was five times higher than that of Whites. Undoubtedly life was harsher in Houston's barrio than in the rest of the city and is reflected in this figure.[7] However, as the effects of the bust dissipated, and as more immigrants moved in, the Latino/Black gap widened considerably after that point and reached the greatest difference in the early 1990s. The gap narrowed yet again a few years later, in 1994. But the Latino rate always remained from two and a half times to four times greater than that of Whites, even as the Latino rate declined. Apparently urban life was relatively tougher for Latinos in Houston than in any other city.

THE UNIQUE CASES

These data provide a rare opportunity to compare the homicides committed by the Mariel Cubans with other segments of the population in Miami. Unfortunately, the data analyzed do not completely distinguish between Cubans and other Latino groups or between Cubans arriving after 1980 (e.g., *Balseros* or boat-rafters), and hence might not provide non-Mariel Cuban-specific rates. For most of the 1980s, Miami Police Department homicide investigators in their coding scheme highlighted Mariel cases. This code is extremely important because it was, and remains, a substantial source of crime information on one of the most negatively perceived immigrant groups in recent history.[8] In addition, homicide tends to be a reliable indicator of the types of violent crime[9] committed by various ethnic groups. This permits some educated speculation on the extent of all Mariel violence.

For most of the 1980s the Miami homicide rate was considerably higher than in the rest of the nation. As mentioned earlier, some of this was attributed to the Marielitos by the popular media and other pundits.[10] If immigration opponents are correct, the appearance of Marielitos should have immediately influenced crime, an effect that should persist even after the initial disruptions in the ethnic communities, and turnovers in populations influenced most by the influx (i.e., Latinos). Therefore, the data presented in figure 6.6 are instructive.

Throughout the early 1980s, there is a temporary upward thrust in homicide rates for the Mariels, countering the declines for all other ethnic groups under consideration. Moreover, from 1981 through 1983, the Mariel homicide rate came very close to that of Blacks, but followed the trends for the rest of the city and fell to a level *lower than* all other groups by the end of the decade. The Mariel Cubans may have had very high rates for a couple of years immediately after their arrival, but by 1990 the number of Mariel killers was so low the detectives stopped singling them out as a separate category.[11] Nevertheless, it is apparent that the Mariel drop paralleled that of Whites in the late 1980s to the point that they were lower than native Whites as the 1990s started.

One immigrant/crime connection is worth making. The Mariel declining homicide rate very closely parallels Roger Lane's[12] discussion of Philadelphia's Italian murder rate in *Murder in America: A History* for the early twentieth century. Italians left a country with the highest homicide rate in Europe and quickly engaged in an "astonishing" homicide rate (26.5 per 100,000). After a few short years, absorption into the workforce, and contact with legitimate opportunities, the Italian homicide rate plunged to 11.4 per 100,000 and eventually fell even farther.[13]

The San Diego data offer a way of comparing native and foreign-born Mexicans in a setting where both were seeking to improve everyday life in the border barrios. The empirical proof also provides further evidence of disparity between immigrants and/or native Latinos compared to other ethnic groups. Again, recall that political advertisements blanketed many media markets with depictions of "illegals" crossing the border into San Diego, overrunning freeways, and committing crime in the local area.[14] According to Richard Lamm,[15] as early as the mid-1970s "the number of maimed illegals and unidentified murdered bodies being brought into the city [of San Diego] from the no-man's-land had gotten too great." This was the result of Mexican and Mexican-American border bandits who preyed on "illegal aliens" trying to cross into San Diego from Mexico. The border bandits "prefer to operate on the American side, in the no-man's-land that the United States has ceded to illegals, their smugglers, and their parasites. American law is so much more lenient, criminals are so much less likely to get beaten up when they are in the custody of the American police." Despite this stereotype regarding criminally inclined Latinos, this city is apparently not overrun with murderous border bandits or their border prey or even Latino killers as a whole.[16] Indeed, as we've seen, Latino homicides are rarely high in San Diego, at least for a city of more than a million residents.

A caveat before turning to figure 6.7 deserves attention. The rare number of border *offenders* required use of border *victims* as a proxy for violent activity associated with "border crossings." To the degree that these are primarily intraracial, and all indications are that this is the case, it is a reliable indicator of the extent of Mexican-origin border activity. These data also are consistently defined. At least since 1960, San Diego Police Department homicide investigators distinguished "Mexican" from other ethnic groups, including non-Mexican Latinos. When possible, they noted the nativity status (foreign-born) to distinguish between foreign and native-born Mexicans and the location of the killing, especially those around border points of entry as well as adjacent areas.

FIGURE 6.6
MARIEL HOMICIDE OFFENDER RATES: ETHNIC TRENDS
AND COMPARISONS

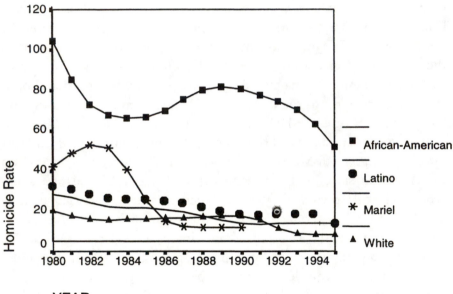

Source: Miami Police Department Homicide Investigation Unit.

FIGURE 6.7
RESIDENT VS. NEW IMMIGRANT LATINOS IN SAN DIEGO, 1985–95

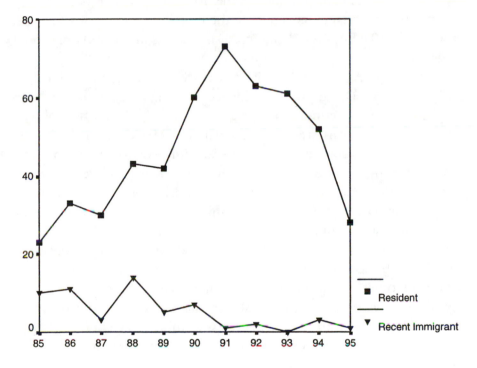

Source: San Diego Police Department Homicide Investigation Unit.

These data suggest a great variety of patterns among the Mexican-origin group, but they, too, are consistent with respect to one feature. Regardless of how high Latino homicides may have been in the barrio or anywhere else in the city of San Diego, homicides on the U.S./Mexican border played a very small role in local violence. As the number of local Mexican killings in figure 6.3 moved up throughout the 1980s and peaked in 1991, the number of border killings remained low and actually declined. The magnitude of the foreign to native-born Latino homicide gap actually spiraled up in the peak "border crossing" period, the mid-1980s. But even then, border homicides numbered only about a dozen.

Overall, these widely publicized instances of immigrant criminals in Miami and San Diego provide evidence of the inaccuracy of stereotyping immigrants as crime-prone (e.g., "Mariel killer" or "border bandit"). Mariel Cubans are not homicidal, and Mexicans on the border are not driven to commit violence. In fact, it is worth pointing out that there are actually some "border bandits," but that they prey on immigrants, not natives, and they account for a small proportion of all homicides in San Diego. Nevertheless, examining the graphs and comparing immigrant Latino homicides to those of older, more established Latinos is highly suggestive. Levels of immigrant Latino homicide involvement are distinctly lower than thought, and in most cases are lower than those of other ethnic groups—both important findings. Both cities probably presented insurmountable obstacles to the adjustment of some newcomers in the area, but even with these difficulties, the impact on homicide, with rare exceptions, was not very different from others in the same area and population.

OFFENDER CHARACTERISTICS: ETHNICITY, GENDER, AND AGE

The detailed annual data analyzed in the preceding section were helpful in that they showed that Latinos did have high offending rates in *very* specific instances, but most were anomalies and exceptions to the overall picture. However, here my concern is with ethnicity, gender, and age. Accordingly, I consider detailed homicide data disaggregated by ethnicity (Black, Latino), age (teen, young and older adults), and gender (male). With these specific tabulations it is possible to compare

Latino males to Black males by age and highlight the groups most likely to engage in homicide.

There are two points to consider before interpreting the homicide data in table 6.1. First, I chose to illustrate this example with 1985 through 1995 homicide rates, which, as we have seen earlier, is the peak of the crack-cocaine epidemic (and the point for which the five-city data are most complete). Second, because the data are average annual rates, they do not reflect extreme fluctuations influenced by a very small number of cases in a given year. Some of the homicide data are based on very small population sizes and are sensitive to changes produced by a handful of cases.

TABLE 6.1
ANNUAL RATES OF HOMICIDE PER 100,000: ETHNICITY, GENDER, AND AGE (1985–95)

Ethnicity, Gender, Age	Chicago	Houston	San Diego	Miami	El Paso
Black origin					
All males	111.1	157.5	36.6	74.2	28.6
13–17	255.5	143.3	94.9	92.2	30.6
18–24	230.0	381.9	162.1	323.9	85.0
25 plus	125.3	131.3	72.7	93.7	30.4
Latino					
All males	43.5	53.6	15.9	16.6	7.1
13–17	52.8	38.0	1.5	8.1	20.5
18–24	87.1	94.5	22.9	38.1	43.7
25 plus	52.6	72.6	25.5	33.5	12.6

Sources: Ethnicity, gender, and age estimates based on data from the U.S. Bureau of the Census. Homicide data are from respective police departments.

Even with that caution in mind, age and gender rates are helpful in comparing these ethnic groups in terms of their concentration in high-crime-prone categories. *In no instance does the average young Latino male exceed or even approach Blacks in their offending rate.* The smallest gap is, however, rather interesting. In El Paso the Black-to-Latino homicide gap is less than in other cities. But even in that case, the El Paso Black male rates (the lowest Black-specific rate in all five cities) are usually one and a half to two times higher than for Latino males.

The position of males in El Paso is not always more favorable than in other cities. In two instances El Paso male rates (teen and young adult) exceed the average San Diego and Miami rate. However, the adult male rate (greater than twenty-five years) is by far the lowest in El Paso. This finding is not entirely unusual, because El Paso occupies a low-end range for both ethnic groups and all five cities in most instances. Overall, the Latino male rates are well behind on the border and in Miami than in Houston and Chicago, and Black offenders exceed even their Latino rates in every case.

LATINOS, BLACKS, HOMICIDE, AND IMMIGRATION

Chapter 2 detailed how immigration has often been highlighted as a critical factor in explaining disorganized communities and high crime rates presumed to be associated with Latinos. As we have already seen, immigration is a logical explanation because it has been a key variable in explaining poverty and homicide of earlier waves of immigrants and migrant Blacks in U.S. history.[17] In fact, as seen in chapter 2, Latino immigration and poverty increased from 1970 to 1990, and the Latino population shifted to being predominantly poor and heavily immigrant. Given the magnitude of this influence, immigration would seem to be a profound factor explaining Latino homicide. The question is whether recent immigration influences levels of homicide within and across these cities.

In a recent study, we examined the impact of recent immigration[18] on Latino and African-American homicides in El Paso, Miami, and San Diego.[19] The results for the Latino models differed somewhat across the three cities, or at least the control variables of population turnover, age, and gender varied. The two most robust findings were for poverty and immigration. High poverty rates were associated with higher levels of Latino homicide, and recent immigration is *unrelated to* Latino homicide, with one exception. The percentage of recent immigrants in the neighborhood is significantly associated with Latino homicide levels only in El Paso, where the direction of this effect is *negative*—that is, areas in El Paso with fewer new immigrants, and presumably more "Americanized," had *higher* Latino homicides, but immigration was not related to higher Latino homicide levels in these three cities.

But despite the finding that the relationship of a community to immigration does not appear to be related to Latino homicides in a consistently direct fashion, Black homicides may have been affected by immigration in these three cities. In fact, the immigration measure is *negatively* related to Black homicide levels in Miami, and *positively* related to Black homicide in San Diego neighborhoods. However, with those noted exceptions, we found a mixed relationship between Black homicides and recent immigration. These results require explanation. First, in Miami, the association between immigration and Black homicides provides support for the argument that neighborhoods with higher proportions of recent immigrants will exhibit lower levels of criminal homicide. Research has found that Haitian immigrants in Miami have suppressed homicide levels in the predominantly Black areas in which they have settled, while Black areas receiving few immigrants continue to have the highest homicide levels in the city. It is worthy of note that Haitians in Miami are among the most disadvantaged groups in the country, experiencing both poverty and discrimination, yet they have exceedingly low homicide involvement.[20]

The exception is the positive effect of immigration on Black homicide in San Diego. One possible interpretation of this result is that homicides in San Diego, those in the center city area in particular, are more likely to involve intergroup conflicts involving new immigrants and Black residents. Another interpretation is that new immigrants tend to settle in San Diego communities with preexisting high levels of Black-on-Black homicide. The latter possibility complements the complex relationships among race/ethnicity, immigration, and crime uncovered by Alba, Logan, and Bellair[21] in their journal article on metropolitan New York. It is plausible that immigrants who settle in predominantly Black neighborhoods are not present in sufficient numbers to strengthen local institutions, and may in fact be contributing to the disorganization of these areas.[22] Further research along these lines would certainly complement recent refinements of social disorganization theory.[23] But it is important not to obscure the general thrust of our results, which in these three border cities does not support either the popular stereotypes of the impact of immigration on crime, or the expectations derived from sociological theories.

The relatively low level of Latino homicide may be surprising to some scholars and pundits. Despite high rates of poverty and high levels of immigration, Latino homicide is lower than might be expected, and this holds in two highly publicized instances (Mariels and border) and for age and gender. This, of course, does not mean that Latinos are not influenced by violence or that crime is not an important feature of Latino populations or communities. It does suggest that public panics or hysteria about some segments of Latino groups are unnecessary.

The available empirical evidence indicates that Blacks in general and Black males in particular—both young and not so young—did indeed fare much worse than Latinos in rates of killing. The gaps shown here are so large that there is little doubt that Latinos are again much less crime-prone than expected, even if the presumed relative rate to Whites is not always particularly favorable.

One prominent finding—that recent immigration does not increase community levels of Latino homicide—has implications for policies that target immigration as a social problem. For example, Section 1 of the controversial Proposition 187 in California declares that residents "have suffered and are suffering personal injury and damage caused by the criminal conduct of illegal aliens in this state."[24] Our results offer little support for claims that immigration facilitates perhaps the most serious form of criminal violence in large and ethnically diverse cities. Indeed, native and immigrant groups alike could profit greatly from research into the counterclaim that immigration can be a stabilizing force that suppresses criminal violence.

Nevertheless, recent violent crime trends remind us that homicides were motivated by circumstances unique to urban America and popularly associated with immigrant Latinos. In the chapter that follows, I show that Latinos were not always immune to changes in the evolution of drug markets, guns, and gangs in U.S. coastal cities.[25] The issue is whether Latinos were influenced at a higher level than the rest of the country. We can reasonably assume that Latino drug activity would be substantially higher if immigrants were involved, since the population includes both foreign and native-born Latinos. In the next chapter I consider the extent of drugs, gangs, robbery, and violent arguments and how they motivated Latinos and Latino homicide.

7. FACT OR FICTION?
Latino Homicide Motives

THE DECEMBER 2000 ISSUE of *The American Enterprise,* a magazine published by the American Enterprise Institute, a conservative Washington, D.C., think tank, features two pictures on the cover that symbolize the "problems" and "solutions" associated with the issue topic "Fixing Our Immigration Predicament." The first picture shows two Latino males throwing gang signs in front of a decaying graffiti-covered wall.[1] The other picture contains six multiethnic youths, presumably White, African American, and Asian, reading college preparatory books. The persistent stereotype of Latino males as gang members in the "problem" photo, especially in an era of record low youth violence rates, and their apparent exclusion in the "solution" photo is remarkable, not the least of which is the lack of any significant writing on crime or gangs in any of the essays and certainly the absence of any analysis on Latino or immigrant crime in the issue. Instead, the magazine cover symbolizes the long-standing stereotype that Latinos are violence-driven and prone to gang violence.

Yet, based on the previous chapter, we now know that an extensive Latino homicide wave never existed, and the instances where rates were high were tied to specific, and in some cases short-lived, circumstances.[2] We also know that a search for high Latino male homicide rates involving youths and young adults did not reveal the "superpredators" some researchers might predict.[3] In addition, we know that the national concern about the rise of "criminal aliens" or hyper "Latino gangbangers" and subsequent responses by politicians across the United States was largely unwarranted. Nevertheless, the cumulative effect of media coverage (intended or not) was to stereotype Latinos as crime-prone.

These overreactions coincided with the rise of urban drug markets in many areas and concern about drug trafficking from abroad, which proliferated in media portrayals of Latinos as criminals on the nightly news and in movies.[4] In fact, images of violent Latinos were as old as the film industry itself.[5] This long-standing representation began with the early *bandito* portrayals in the silent-screen Westerns, shifting to more urban settings in the 1960s and 1970s, with images of switchblade-carrying juvenile delinquents, as in *West Side Story*. The stereotypes continued throughout the 1980s and 1990s in depictions of Latino gang members, violent criminals, and drug lords in reality-based television series such as *Cops* and *America Undercover,* and in recent popular films.[6] For example, the movie *Scarface* (1983) features "Tony Montana," a coke-snorting Mariel refugee battling Colombians and Cubans over the Miami drug trade and engaging in gruesome violence. Similar acts of violence are contained in *Carlito's Way* (1993), a movie involving Carlito Brigante, a reformed drug dealer from Spanish Harlem trying to elude his Puerto Rican friends who are determined to pull him back into a life of crime. In *American Me,* another film focusing exclusively on Latino gangs, the main characters are members of the Mexican Mafia, a prison gang, and participate in wanton violence, including killing siblings for violating gang orders. All three films, in general, negatively portray Latinos as tough street thugs speaking accented English, highlighting again the stereotypical image of a violence-prone and drug-centered group, much like that of the characters on the cover of conservative periodicals.[7] The issue is whether this imagery is based in fact or is rather the continuation of an old typecast.

To explore this question, the current chapter focuses on Latino-specific circumstances.[8] Using previous homicide research as a guide, I obtained Latino homicide motive data (e.g., gang, drug, intimate, escalation, or robbery killings), and the following analysis concentrates on those cases. As we saw in the previous chapter, Latinos played a small role in the youth violence epidemic, but that might not necessarily correspond to drug- or gang-related homicides. Moreover, the following Latino findings parallel some *national* levels, not just city-specific rates, which serves as a reminder that Latinos were rarely in *any* high-rate category.

The previous chapter found some exceptions to this trend, and unusual patterns will be addressed here as well. For example, people writing about Miami's drug scene writers in the early 1980s focused on the involvement of the Mariel Cubans,[9] while reports on those of Mexican origin in Houston displayed homicide levels in line with similarly situated African Americans, so comparisons will be made for these two anomalies. Nevertheless, a thorough examination of homicide motivations is necessary to remind us that city wide increases are not always linked to Latinos, even though the public imagination might link them to drugs, gangs, or killings of loved ones.

BACKGROUND

There is one technical matter to resolve before comparing the circumstances of Latino homicides. My access to complete and detailed homicide circumstance information in *all* five cities is limited to the 1985 through 1995 years.[10] This is not a major obstacle, since the bulk of gang and drug activities occurred throughout this period.[11] If the data were pushed back in time, most of these incidents would highlight the mundane initiation of homicide (e.g., arguments and robberies turned lethal, or killings between intimates). Other incidents document the rise of drug- and gang-motivated killings, with some exceptions. The noted exceptions are analyzed later in this chapter.

It has been documented that battles over drug markets contributed to high violent crime rates in urban America.[12] Scholars also have demonstrated that the reemergence of gang activity meant that homicide proportions rose simultaneously with drug-related killings.[13] These two homicide types (gang/drug) combined with machismo, honor, and disrespect, were always persistent factors contributing to homicide in escalation and intimate circumstances.

Nevertheless, those were not the only factors shaping homicide. The economy faltered at times in the 1980s and 1990s, leaving many urban residents in neighborhoods that were unable to regulate street interactions between males, or provide sustained economic growth, which contributed to more attractive targets for lethal robberies and opportunities to create illegal enterprises.[14] Jacqueline Cohen and colleagues, in a recent article "The Role of Drug Markets and Gangs in Local Homicide Rates," describe how social control in many communities deteriorated to the point that conventional institutions—jobs, schools, churches—fled in the wake of urban disorder, contributing to violence in areas where deviant markets filled the void left by legitimate businesses. They remark,[15] "Obvious market features of illegal drug and gang activities contribute directly to violence associated with these enterprises. A number of distinct features of crack markets—for example, entry of a new and lucrative product sold by new and often inexperienced dealers in an unregulated market—promote high levels of fierce competition for market shares among potential dealers. Dealers in these illegal cash markets, who have no recourse to conventional civil or criminal law enforcement protections, also represent very attractive targets for robbery. In the absence of conventional and peaceful means for resolving market disputes, participants in these enterprises often resort to violence as a means of protecting their market positions." Whatever the explanation for increased homicides in some ethnic groups, the rate of Latino incidents varied, suggesting that the distinct motivation behind each killing requires attention. After all, some levels rose, others fell, and some remained constant.

LATINO HOMICIDE MOTIVATIONS AND CIRCUMSTANCES

Even though America's Black youths and young adults experienced a twofold and fourfold increase in homicide risk, this connection did not necessarily correspond to Latino trends.[16] As we will see, the Latino circumstances varied substantially in these five cities, and pointing to the rise in crack markets and gangs to explain Latino violence is potentially misleading. This does not mean that gangs and drug-related violence were *not* problems in Latino communities—gang conflicts as well as some struggles over drug markets had been a problem for years in southern California.[17] It is also true that Latino gang and drug violence did worsen over the years under investigation but again, these activities increased across most of urban America and reflect some of the routine experiences Blacks and Latinos encountered daily.

To a large extent, Latino homicide also varies by motivation, and city-specific circumstances (indirectly influenced by immigration) were powerful forces in explaining the shifting lethal activity among Latinos, which in a few isolated instances approached high-rate levels. The primary motivation contributing to a homicide is but one example of social exchanges swaying violence, accelerating and decreasing in response to local conditions.[18] Incidents occurring in the course of an argument, typically arising out of routine disputes into a lethal event, heavily shaped homicides in the mid- to late 1980s and beyond in a few cases. These features were not directly linked to gang-related offenses or altercations over drug-trafficking markets, although both were undoubtedly routine components of the social milieu, but were enduring and widespread components of exchanges requiring physical responses to challenges between individuals.[19]

Figures 7.1 through 7.5 present the annual homicide rate for killings that were drug-, escalation-, gang-, intimate-, or robbery-motivated. The figures are city-specific to facilitate comparing the circumstances in changes across time. The longitudinal patterns differ, but similarities also appear. In 1985, escalation among Latinos was the primary homicide motivation in Chicago, Houston, Miami, and San Diego, and was the second-leading type in El Paso. The rate of disputes that turned lethal decreased sharply in Houston and Miami but persisted at the same level in Chicago, rose and fell in San Diego, and increased slightly in El Paso. These swings indicate that local conditions matter, since some Latinos experienced economic downswings, such as the loss of a well-paying, low-skill job. The swings also indicate that motivations are better indicators of trends than aggregated national statistics that obscure important area characteristics.

Substantial differences do exist in the base rate of gang/drug homicides across the five cities, which increase in some instances throughout the ten-year period, but rarely in a uniform manner. Gang-related homicides in Chicago accelerated over the time frame and are still on the rise, but drug-motivated killings remained remarkably low in figure 7.4. Not surprisingly, gang-related killings after 1985 exhibited a fivefold increase at the national level, and Chicago also might reflect the role of gang retaliations and other activity during this period.[20] Even though the Chicago upsurge was much slower than at the national level, at least according to official definitions, gang violence turning lethal was clearly on the rise.

Both drug- and gang-motivated homicides, however, were rare in El Paso and Houston. But again, caution is necessary when viewing the figures, since these events were uncommon, causing upward swings when a small number were added to the population count. The two

FIGURE 7.1

MIAMI LATINO HOMICIDE MOTIVES, 1985–95

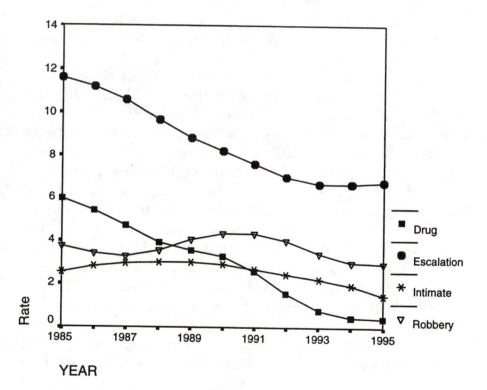

Source: Miami Police Department Homicide Investigation Unit.

FIGURE 7.2
EL PASO LATINO HOMICIDE MOTIVES, 1985–94

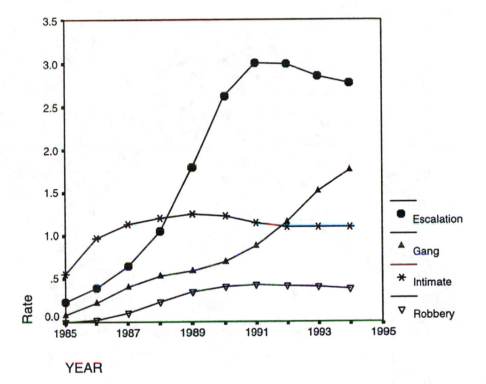

Source: El Paso Police Department Homicide Investigation Unit.

FIGURE 7.3
SAN DIEGO LATINO HOMICIDE MOTIVES, 1985–95

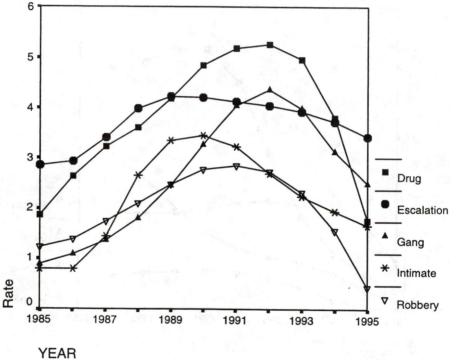

Source: San Diego Police Department Homicide Investigation Unit.

FIGURE 7.4
CHICAGO LATINO HOMICIDE MOTIVES, 1985–94

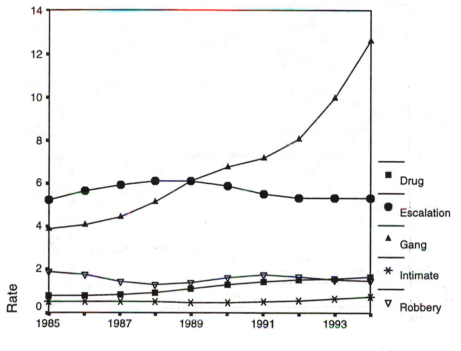

Source: Homicide in Chicago, 1965–1995.

FIGURE 7.5
HOUSTON LATINO HOMICIDE MOTIVES, 1985–94

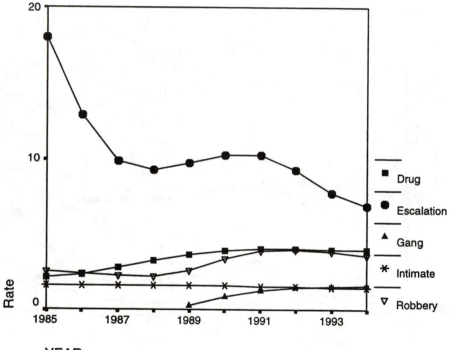

Source: Houston Police Department Homicide Investigation Unit.

Texas cities' drug rate grew slightly, but to a degree less than escalation rates. While El Paso maintained a very low gang rate, for all intents and purposes the drug-related level was nonexistent. Gang-related homicides did double over a very short time, but still involved extremely rare events in El Paso, with changes in a handful of cases artificially skewing the rate. Regardless of the fact that the gang motivation rose, the base rate was persistently lower than for cities with the same population size.

In Miami, drug-related homicides were not only a leading motivation contributing to Latino killings but also a prominent factor contributing to violence throughout the city in the early 1980s.[21] However, while Miami's drug-associated killings were higher initially than in other cities, drug-related homicides plummeted to a level that barely merits attention at the end of this time frame. This is not to suggest that illegal drug activities did not contribute to Latino illegality and violence. In fact, dealers and buyers generated rampant violence and retaliations, but the rates were lower than in the rest of country and actually preceded the national crack cocaine epidemic.[22] Consider also that Miami never had the street gang tradition endemic in other old and large cities on the West and East Coasts, where "turf wars" were much more prominent. Much of the street aggression over drugs occurred among small groups of loosely knit persons engaging in low-level street activities.

Figure 7.3 suggests that the high concentration of Latino homicide from 1988 through 1994 made San Diego a dangerous place for Latinos. Unlike the other cities, *all* types of homicide motivation rose simultaneously, with drug types peaking at a rate higher than gang and escalation motives, but most intersecting from about 1990 through 1992. It is also worth noting that killings between intimates and in the course of a robbery also spiked during a similar interval. Thus local circumstances such as a declining defense economy permitted Latino homicides to temporarily spiral up, but higher-than-average Latino rates rarely emerged in the already low homicide context of San Diego.

Whatever the specific motivations behind homicide, it is the predictable presence of intimate (almost exclusively male on female) and robbery (heavily stranger-involved) homicides that is perhaps the most lasting characteristic in all of the figures. Both types were sustained by very different circumstances over time. Unlike gang or drug motivations, intimate and robbery homicides have consistently been characterized by social interactions between lovers (or ex-lovers) or unknown intruders, respectively, that are a constant feature of events that turn lethal.[23]

Riedel and Best[24] provide one of the most current discussions of intimate homicides. People kill loved ones during an intense argument driven by lust, rage, jealousy, or a host of other emotions tied to close sexual relationships. Frustration and conflict are routine in many relationships, but those that turn violent and eventually lethal are also shaped by power, betrayal, and control. Therefore, intimate homicides occur between people who love (or loved) one another, resulting in circumstances heavily victimizing females. Another Miami police record speaks to this: "The body of Dolores Rodriguez lay on the sidewalk in front of 'The Club Oh La La'—a place she worked as a barmaid in an intersection on the Miami River concentrated with several fish markets, marine supply companies, boat docks, bars, and restaurants. According to the owner, Ms. Rodriguez was involved with two "pescadores" or fishermen but had recently broken up with one of them. Up until a couple of weeks ago, she frequently showed up at work with a bloody lip or black eye. Apparently her boyfriend 'Mario Carballo' would beat her when she arrived home from work late, accusing her of flirting too much with customers, an effort he would view from outside the open air bar.

"Dolores came into the bar one day and gave her two weeks notice. Tired of his abuse, she had left Mario for 'Juan Ortega,' another bar patron, and they would soon start a new life together in Key West, where Juan's brother had his own fishing boat. Still, she was very concerned for her safety. Juan swore revenge and wanted to get even with Mario for 'what he had done to his girlfriend,' and Mario still followed her home from work late at night. She wanted to leave town as quickly as possible but needed to work and save her tips to help pay for the move to Key West. Her concern was warranted. The next night, both Mario and Juan showed up at the bar while Dolores was working. A verbal altercation between the two occurred and the bar owner told them to take it outside, otherwise he was going to call the police. According to witnesses, Juan told Mario, "I'm going to do to you what you did to her" and punched and kicked him until his body rolled into the street. Mario ran away and left. The bar owner asked Juan to leave while Dolores finished her shift since 'he didn't want any more trouble' in his bar. Juan agreed. As the night wore on, the excitement of the fight wore down, and the bar closed. As the owner and Dolores left the bar, Mario appeared out of the shadows, yelled, "If I can't have her nobody can," and shot her twice in the chest. She died immediately, and Mario was caught hiding in some bushes under a drawbridge two blocks away."

In the case of robbery homicide, scholars typically agree that some areas are better able to control violence than others. A few are less able to protect street targets, and provide some opportunities for violent confrontations.[25] In part this is because some communities have greater numbers of transients, or temporary residents such as tourists or military personnel and are less able to protect themselves from strangers or discourage violence that shapes some urban areas.[26] Take the robbery-motivated killings in an isolated business area with no residents adjacent to downtown Miami: "The robbery took place at the 'Little Havana Auto Parts Store,' which was closer to downtown than Little Havana. Multiple shots had been heard but few witnesses were around since it was past closing time on a Sunday night and most of the surrounding businesses—a pawnshop, junkyard, wrecker service, and check-cashing place—were long closed. To complicate matters, a nearby highway was undergoing construction, and cement barriers and cranes were surrounding the block, further isolating it from the rest of the area. A radio dispatcher at the junkyard had heard several shots fired but saw nothing, since he was inside the office. As the detectives showed up at the auto parts store, several puddles of blood were in the parking lot and two bodies were lying on the concrete next to a Nissan Pathfinder (which had been stolen). A register cash drawer with money was also in the car. With few witnesses, at least for the moment, it appeared several people were involved. With the help of forensic experts, some reconstruction, and the store security camera, it appeared the owner had been robbed as he was closing the store. Three armed people went inside, ordered him to open the cash register, which they then took outside to a waiting car. The owner reached under his counter, got his gun out, and went outside. Apparently several shots were fired; the storeowner and one of the robbers were killed. The others got away, apparently fleeing to a nearby metro stop and escaping on the train. No money had been taken, and the co-offenders were never caught."

Most killings develop from routine incidents, as opposed to primarily drug and gang events, as the following elaboration of escalation killings demonstrates. The rate of escalation homicide was consistently high, if not the highest, in these five figures. Exceptions are noted, yet during the period under study the cities were routinely influenced by lethal arguments. In some cities these differences were massive, although the reader should recognize that most cities had low Latino rates, and increases reflect a small number of cases propelling the rate up.

THE EXCEPTIONS REVISITED

The assertion that Latinos represent a significant source of drug/gang violence or intimate killings, as the "macho" stereotype suggests, is less than valid in the current analysis. This study set out to explore these dynamics, and I found that regardless of motivation and time, high Latino homicide levels were anomalies. The following discussion highlights the benefits of examining two high-rate cases, Miami throughout the 1980s and Houston in the early 1980s. As Cecilia Menjivar[27] notes, examining unusual cases in detail presents "unique opportunities to rework explanations of normal ones." In other words, the stories that follow help shed light on Latino homicides more generally, since they illustrate that local conditions matter more than ethnicity, and that Latinos were just as sinned against as they were sinners when all ethnic groups were considered.[28]

Mariels in Miami

It is important to recognize that homicides were high in Miami in the early 1980s and that this effect carried through much of that decade. As Inciardi and colleagues[29] note, "although Miami received international attention during the early 1980s because of the number of drug-related homicides, much has changed in the years since," including a struggle over cocaine distribution networks. Cubans were perceived as local brokers or middlemen, and impressionistic data seem to indicate that Mariel Cubans bore the brunt of this experience and that other ethnic groups differed in this regard from the newcomers. It is almost certain that a wide variety of local problems were attributed to the "Marielitos," and drug-related violence was central among them. For example, in addition to drug-motivated homicides, the local newspapers blamed the Mariels for several high-profile crime waves in the summer and fall of 1980.[30] Youth crimes, gang violence, and other random acts of street violence were soon defined as Mariel crime, cementing their violent image in the local imagination.[31]

TABLE 7.1

DRUG- AND NONDRUG-RELATED HOMICIDES BY ETHNICITY:
CITY OF MIAMI, 1980–90 (N = 2,119)

Homicides	Anglos	African Americans	Mariel Latinos	Cubans
Nondrug (%)	89.2	84.1	84.1	82.9
Drug (%)	10.8	15.9	15.9	17.1

Source: City of Miami Police Department homicide supplemental reports, 1980–90.
Note: Total number of cases based on known motivation. The "Latinos" definition is non-Mariel-specific in this column.

Table 7.1 shows the percentage of drug- and nondrug-related homicides by ethnicity from 1980 through 1990. The rows give the actual percentage in the ethnicity category for Anglos, African Americans, Latinos (or at least non-Mariel Latinos), and Mariel Cubans. These figures show that all groups were comparably involved in drug-related homicides. Consider, for example, the Anglo comparisons. About 16 to 17 percent of all homicides were attributed to some type of drug involvement in the African-American, Latino, and Mariel Cuban groups. This is higher than for Anglos, but even the largest gap (Anglo to Mariel) is only 6.3 percent. Some discrepancy in these figures would be expected, since some homicides were not solved, but even then, little evidence exists that these would significantly vary by ethnicity, given that the vast majority were solved and committed by fellow group members.[32]

By contrast, a look at the non-drug homicides can give a clue as to how much of Miami's homicide was not attributed to fights over drugs or drug market activity. Consider that about 83 to about 89 percent of all homicides with known circumstances were not connected to drug activity. In each case there was little evidence that *any* ethnic group was excessively involved in drug-related killings. It is almost certain that myth, not fact, gave rise to the "new" legacy of Scarface.

Chicanos in Houston

Houston's high homicide rate between 1980 and 1985, as well as the sharp drop experienced after those years in what had until then been a narrow Black/Latino homicide gap, covers a rather interesting period.

The "oil bust" and the years immediately following it probably affected the homicide rate of Latinos as the service sector experienced a decline and construction jobs disappeared.[33] It was only in about 1985 that the Latino rate started to drop; after a few years it dropped much more. The types of homicide could sharpen the picture of why much of the change in Latino violence took place at that time rather than later, or on into the 1990s. Hence it is possible that drug and gang violence was high, since alternatives to work were few, and the shifts in homicide rates reflected a change that *should* have taken place well into the 1980s and 1990s, since opportunities to mature out of gangs and illegal activities evaporated.[34] If the violent shifts and fluctuations in the local economy during this period affected Blacks and Latinos differently, then this would have some bearing on homicide circumstances in these ethnic groups.

In the early 1980s a substantial fraction of Latino killings—almost 40 percent—were related to an argument. Hence, relative to Blacks and Whites, at the very height of the oil bust cycle, almost half of Latinos were killed in settings that arose out of an altercation of some type, but not gang- or drug-related. For example, the escalation percentages were lower for the other two groups (which also show some variation), but Blacks and Whites had higher robbery, felony, and intimate homicides. Thus the period covered was marked by high rates of escalation killings, which were differentially experienced by ethnic groups and had a serious bearing on Latino homicide.

Certainly, other factors probably influenced Latino homicides, but the expected discovery of drug or gang involvement never emerged. The higher gap for Latino escalation homicides is expected because of the consequences of downsizing, but that never translated to high levels in other homicide types. Other ethnic groups turned to robbery or intimate killings in this period, but there is no comparable high Latino fraction.

It is another question as to why the Latino experience during the late 1980s and early 1990s was not as severe as that experienced by Whites and Blacks in the same city. Moreover, it is not possible with these data to determine whether there were annual changes in unemployment before 1980 or in the 1980–84 period. However, the data suggest that the remarkable Latino peaks observed in Miami and Houston occurred during a period of local turmoil, and all ethnic groups

TABLE 7.2
CITY OF HOUSTON: TYPES OF HOMICIDE MOTIVES, 1980–84 (N = 1,699)

Primary Motivation	Anglos	Latinos	African Americans
Drug (%)	2.3	1.9	4.1
Intimate (%)	16.8	13.9	35.3
Escalation (%)	37.3	48.2	33.9
Robbery (%)	20.7	14.3	9.6
Gang (%)	0.2	0.3	0.0
Felony (%)	7.5	5.6	8.8
Other (%)	15.1	15.6	8.4

Source: City of Houston UCR supplemental homicide records.
Note: Total number of cases based on known motivation.

were radically influenced by these changes. The Latino impact could have been predicted, yet it was short-lived and tied to specific social conditions that would be expected to affect any group.

Why was the typical participation of Latinos in drug and gang homicides so low? The greater concentration of Latinos in urban centers with well-known gang traditions and drug trafficking routes is in no small way a major source of their stereotypes over other groups, a situational factor that should work to their disadvantage. Thus, if the crime-prone image should appear, especially when compared to other crime types, the results should have demonstrated that level in this chapter. Nevertheless, it is clear at this point that with rare exceptions, Latinos have not manifested that trend. In other words, differences in the propensity of drug, gang, intimate, or argument killings, or temporal shifts in the unique cases, are not directly related to changes in immigration (as in the Mariels) but linked more directly to local conditions.

There is instead clear evidence that Latinos are resilient and will reside in cities and neighborhoods where homicide is relatively low despite adverse community conditions. To be sure, there is no denying that exceptions have occurred in this chapter and previous ones; rather than being a rule, it is typically a question of relative degree when compared with similarly situated groups or extreme circumstances. We should expect that Latino neighborhoods have uniformly high rates, but the lesson is that resilience is the rule, not the exception.

8. CONCLUSION
Moving beyond Black and White Violent Crime Research

AMERICAN CITIES ARE NOW radically different from those on which social scientists based their models and theories of urban life, at least since the decade preceding World War II.[1] The traditional urban experience was captured by transformations[2] associated with waves of European immigrants and southern Black migrants.[3] It was predominantly midwestern and northeastern cities that attracted foreign and native-born newcomers and became home to a new population of Black and White residents studied by early social scientists.[4] Regarding the "new" Americans, scholars debated social policy largely in terms of what worked for Whites and Blacks, or didn't, and framed questions and answers in racial dichotomies.[5]

But today, Latino immigration has given rise to diverse, multiethnic American cities, creating new immigrant-serving enterprises and revitalizing impoverished barrios, some in communities that had been predominantly Latino for several generations.[6] Social analysis in strictly Black and White categories is no longer able to capture the true nature and extent of ethnicity in contemporary urban life, a notion with particular relevance for studies on the causes and consequences of urban crime. Moreover, the burgeoning populations of immigrants and Latinos led some to conclude that the scope of Latino crime had expanded and that Latinos should have similar impacts as turn-of-the-twentieth-century immigrants, or at least should have experienced crime in the same fashion as other poor ethnic minority groups in contemporary

America.[7] Although the Latino population has grown, why hasn't it suffered this fate?

In this book I have sought to explore Latino homicides in five cities—rather different venues than those studied by earlier social scientists, but ones that reflect where Latinos now reside and others attempt to reach through legal and not so legal means. In a country where Latinos are a prominent ethnic minority group and where population shifts to Sunbelt cities have encouraged a new urban spirit, Latinos (recent and old) have established new communities, maintained older ones, and in the process reconfigured local conditions by creating a presence where none existed.[8]

Furthermore, this book places Latinos at the center of criminological research. It does not lump Latinos with other "non-White" ethnic groups, nor does it treat them as one of a series of control variables in a statistical analysis. Instead I emphasize the legacy of earlier settlement patterns, contemporary local conditions, and relative homicide experiences within Latino groups and to other ethnic groups. I also integrate previous immigration research and current scholarship on Latino crime in urban America. As James F. Short Jr.[9] notes, "Each city has its own special history, and what works in one city might not work in another. There is no substitute for local knowledge, including both up-to-date information and an appreciation of history." Working within this tradition, I found that while the local conditions producing Latino criminal activity are complex, Latinos are not as criminally involved as expected, at least as measured by the serious crime of homicide.

EFFECTS OF ECONOMIC DEPRIVATION AND IMMIGRATION

When I began this study it seemed logical that poverty and immigration would shape Latino homicides in all five cities. They have long settled in impoverished areas, and some continued to arrive in well-established barrios or enclaves. Also, many entered during a period when immigrants were singled out for discrimination, blamed for a host of social problems, and presumably seemed to embody the characteristics of a crime-prone group, one that is both highly victimized and engaged in offending. Latinos, regardless of citizenship, were rarely welcomed with open arms in any of these cities, and in some there exists a long history of exclusion and isolation.[10]

According to the conventional view, poverty should increase homicides as immigrant Latino populations expand and as established group members are socialized into the local "code of the streets" and penetrate beyond the initial settlement points.[11] However, as detailed in the previous chapters, that is not typically the case. Contrary to what the criminological literature proposes, Latino immigration has not led to disproportionate levels of homicide because *Latinos are poor but working*, albeit in low-paying jobs in both the formal and informal sectors. To be sure, there were some exceptions when Latino homicides rose and some impoverished Latino communities suffered from the ravages of drug- and gang-related violence. But even in those instances the rates were usually not as striking when compared to citywide or community-wide levels or other ethnic minority groups.

Although arguments about the impact of poverty on homicide are reasonable and important, a more explicit explanation means that increased poverty rates per se do not hold the key to Latino homicide findings. More precisely, *relative deprivation*[12] and *structural conditions*[13] provide a compelling explanation of Latino homicide. Poverty is often rampant in the barrio and enclave for native and foreign-born Latinos, but expectations are low, given even worse conditions that some Latinos experienced in the home country or that others routinely view from the confines of the border.[14] Acknowledging these effects permits me to explain why Latino homicides are suppressed and thereby offers a more complete explanation of Latino crime. While these factors independently can affect Latino homicide rates, it is the convergence of these two conditions that has deflected homicides—at the individual and community levels. I begin by turning to the structural explanation in the following section and return to relative deprivation in the next section.

Structural and Relative Deprivation Explanations

The Latino case exemplifies a consistent finding of urban sociologists: Attachments to the world of work, even through subsistence-paying jobs, are part of the bond that fortifies Latino communities and helps them absorb the shock of widespread poverty. However, it also demonstrates an accompanying connection to violent crime that has not been fully explored to this point. Unstable, poorly paid jobs requiring few skills are not easily obtained without assistance, be they in the barrio, enclave, or elsewhere. Instead, the process of seeking, receiving, and providing employment demands access to a variety of resources[15] that are not always readily available in ethnic minority communities. In its place, many mediating institutions—families, friends, schools, work, and church—provide entrée to the service sector. This does not necessarily guarantee upward mobility or even minimal pay for Latinos, but it does influence crime by "short-circuiting" the poverty/homicide connection to a greater extent than for similarly situated non-Latinos.[16]

Although some aspects of the Latino immigration experience suggest a replication of the past, or at least a romanticized notion of earlier immigration, a few differences stand out.[17] Foremost, Latinos are being absorbed into a world of servitude or of providing services to employers in search of workers willing to labor for low pay. This is not the growing industrial economy of manufacturing jobs requiring hard work but few skills, encountered by those moving through Ellis Island a hundred years ago.[18] Of course, not everyone went to well-paying jobs at the turn of the twentieth century; many toiled in dangerous coal mines or poorly paid steel mills and rural farms. Yet the contrast is that Latinos are entering a service segment that is relatively poorer than a hundred years ago, are far less favorably received and much less integrated into society than most Europeans, then or now.[19] Furthermore, working-class European immigrants at the turn of the twentieth century labored in an economy that allowed them as well as their European predecessors and children to move up and out into the middle class. The social and economic context facing Latino (and other nonwhite) immigrants is drastically different in contemporary society. Racial discrimination still exists, and labor market barriers to well-paying jobs flourish.[20]

With that caveat in mind and as I just noted, job attachments partially explain the mystery of why Latino immigrants are not as criminally involved as popularly portrayed and why Latino violence is low. Not only are job attachments in the United States better than in the country of origin, suggesting a variant on relative deprivation, but also there is plenty of evidence that opportunities for low-paying employment exist, usually with coethnics and mostly located in barrios or enclaves with previous compatriots.[21] Ethnic connections within Latino communities provide the foundation for formal and informal structures that lead to information and support in acquiring skills and eventually work. Thus the story of immigration is largely the story of ethnic niches and social networks binding new migrants with nonmigrants and older ones.[22] This helps explain why both the Mariel Cubans in Miami and Mexican border crossers took significant steps up from Third World poverty in such a short time, rarely participated in violence, and even more importantly why many poor and immigrant Latino communities have low homicide rates.

A related issue, and one closely connected to social capital,[23] is how economic and political refugees from abroad influenced immigration and crime.[24] Many Latinos left war-torn countries and totalitarian regimes throughout the 1980s and settled in the United States. Some were persecuted for political reasons, especially for membership in opposing political groups, and in many cases were victims of official violence themselves. Others left in search of jobs and better wages. The majority of both refugee groups, however, had to *enter* the United States without the benefits of legality (which I discuss in the last section of this chapter). This meant planning a long trip; gathering resources to carry it out; crossing at least one border (and in many instances two or three); amassing and carrying relatively large sums of money; and, of course, exposure to enormous personal dangers during the journey to the United States.[25] As Cecilia Menjivar[26] eloquently states: "When refugee immigrants make use of social webs similar to those used by *regular* immigrants to reach their destinations, it becomes difficult to disentangle whether they are *political* or *economic* migrants [my emphasis]." Thus immigration, as it affects other aspects of an individual's experience and community conditions, is probably not influenced by immigrant status in and of itself. The key variable is the effect of conditions in the receiving local context, including an individual's social capital, as well as discrimination, punitive government reactions, etc., since the circumstances driving such as person from home have more similarities than is commonly recognized.

Furthermore, as one example of the influence of conditions in different regions of the receiving country, I discuss the high-crime context of South Florida compared with the low-crime context of West Texas in terms of implications for the groups who settled in these areas.[27] While Miami's Latino population received government support related to their status as "political" exiles, Mexican immigrants were presumably motivated primarily by economic factors (as in El Paso) and have not received such assistance.[28] Certainly if they did obtain any support, it did not trickle down to the barrio. Nevertheless, according to traditional theories of violence, this lack of aid, exposure to militarylike conditions, social isolation, and extremely high rates of poverty on the border should result in higher rates of homicide in El Paso communities than in similarly sized cities such as Miami (for perspective, see Archer and Gartner 1984). Yet the opposite was found to be true at the city and community levels.[29]

ETHNIC COMPARISONS
AND COMPARABLE CONDITIONS

The primary point of this study was not to portray Latinos in general, or immigrants in particular, as more or less criminal or crime-prone than Whites or Blacks, but rather to acknowledge that important ethnic group differences exist and that Latinos should be studied separately from other racial/ethnic groups. More importantly, we should avoid media-influenced "moral panics"—attitudes that belie the facts presented throughout this book. However, important Black/Latino differences did emerge and require explanation. The obstacles faced by Blacks and Latinos in these five cites were enormous, and in many cases, such as the level of poverty, comparable to each other. That is to say, rough economic comparability exists in terms of poverty rates, but there also are important historical and current differences in treatment. Simply stated, the African-American rate is higher because their history (including the legacy of slavery) is very different from the Latino history of discrimination in this country.

Relative deprivation, both to similarly situated ethnic minority groups and to conditions in the home country, also accounts for Latino homicide patterns. For example, there is no doubt that historically, Blacks were singled out far more intensely than Latinos in these five cities, and contemporary domains (e.g., economic and political) of everyday life still reflect that legacy. Witness, for example, the numerous riots in reaction to police brutality in Miami and Los Angeles; the lack of investment in many of Miami's Black-dominated neighborhoods such as Liberty City and Overtown; and certainly a perception that

Blacks are underrepresented in the political arena relative to Latinos and that when they do vote, their votes don't count.

Maybe there is less racism toward Latinos than toward African Americans? This might translate to fewer hurdles in gaining low-paying jobs from small employers or access to the informal economy, providing some temporary relief and stability, which, in turn, influence social problems, including crime. Furthermore, racial barriers are now more permeable than in the past and there is probably less overt racism toward both Blacks and Latinos than a generation ago. Civil rights leaders, especially African Americans, made these advances, and Latinos to a large extent also have benefited from those actions.

These facts cannot be glossed over, as they are central to my contention that *Latinos have lower homicide rates than African Americans because they exhibit higher levels of social integration, especially as measured by labor market involvement.* Again, my argument is that the Latino homicide rate is lower because of employment differences and differences in mediating institutions, where the functionality of the latter is tied intimately to the social processes surrounding getting here successfully. This raises at least two questions about ethnicity and homicide: If Blacks did have greater obstacles, to what degree was this barrier the result of local conditions? Second, if ethnicity is important, how does one reconcile the fact that Latino homicide rates are in line with those of Whites in some instances?

The data comparing Black and Latino conditions in the introduction and in chapter 3 provide a clear conclusion to the first question. The conditions that Blacks and Latinos face are extremely poor, and both groups' initial entry point into American society is probably uniformly low relative to that of Whites, even in cities that are predominantly Latino or majority minority in population composition. However, it is an error to assume that Latino conditions are as "bad" as those of Blacks *over and above poverty* or that Blacks have a "cultural" or "genetic" deficiency requiring attention. The situation for Latinos, devastating as it is in many barrios, is not as bad in terms of concentrated unemployment and joblessness as for African Americans. Witness, for example, the differences in table 1 in the first chapter; the greater involvement of Blacks in homicide rates; drug- and gang-related homicides (consequences of male joblessness) alluded to in chapters 4 and 6 and noted by others; and even the lack of immigration into many urban poor Black neighborhoods, a factor that seems to have fortified Latino communities. Immigration did drive up the Latino poverty rate, but it also strengthened communities by replacing those who moved out, widening the circle of formal and informal ties to work, and creating or extending niches that served *all* Latinos.

An important point to revisit, and one that others should consider when expanding research on economic conditions and crime, is that factors shaping Latino poverty are broader and more varied than accounted for in traditional types of quantitative analyses. That is, other than influencing poverty rates, an influx of poor immigrant Latinos has a profound effect on earlier arrivals and long-standing residents from the same group. Resumption of large-scale immigration and continued concentration in border areas facilitate certain perceptions or at least frames of reference regarding Latino poverty or relative deprivation that other ethnic groups might not encounter. In other words, immigrant Latinos have routine contact with the old country, and the negative consequences of poverty in the barrio or enclave, relative to that in Cuba, Mexico, El Salvador, Nicaragua, or even Puerto Rico, might not appear as difficult to overcome or at least endure. Violence and poverty in countries where civil strife is common are much different and much more intimidating than what one confronts here in the United States. Again, this is a broad application of the concept of relative deprivation but an important twist on notions of transnational poverty that requires more attention in the future.[30]

Moreover, life in barrios such as San Ysidro (San Diego) or El Segundo Barrio (El Paso) might seem less harmful than that of Tijuana or Ciudad Juarez, which are within plain sight of residents on the U.S. side of the border. As a result, when new and old Latino immigrants think of the impoverished conditions they face here, appalling as they may be in most of the twenty communities detailed in chapter 4, poverty back home, where they have constant contacts because there are continued influxes, is probably much worse. Immigrants in their daily negotiations with work, settlement, and everyday life in general perceive their new status as infinitely better than where they came from.[31]

The answer to the second question is much more elusive. Again, how do we explain the reality of similar Latino and White homicide rates in some cases? Although systematic quantitative data are not fully available, there is reason to believe that if non-Latino White poverty and Latino poverty were comparable, White rates might *surpass* those of Latinos. This is not an unusual situation. Recall historical evidence when Italians had higher homicide rates than Blacks in Philadelphia at the turn of the twentieth century.[32] Remember also that non-Latino White data are hard to come by, since many Latinos classify themselves as "racially" White (or other races) but ethnically Latino. Nevertheless, these data are suggestive, since they provide some clarification on non-Latino White and Latino homicide differences (or similarities, as in post-1980 Miami and El Paso). At the metropolitan and city levels, Whites in El Paso and Miami (two predominantly Latino cities where Latino homicide rates resembled those of Whites at certain points in chapter 5) had a slightly lower rate of poverty than Latinos (about 25 percent for Whites, to 30 percent for Latinos). But Whites had an *average per capita income* several thousand dollars higher than Latinos. This, of course, might be skewed due to a greater concentration of White elites versus Latino elites; political empowerment; center city/ suburbanlike residence; and, of course, relative starting point, among other factors. Nevertheless, it is worth noting that the advantages of immigration should be explored in more detail in the future so that scholars better understand how Latinos, a heavily immigrant group faced with adverse conditions, seem to endure violent crime better than native-born groups.[33]

POLICY IMPLICATIONS

The assumption that poor ethnic minorities, whether they are Latino immigrants or Latinos in general, are uniformly crime-prone deserves reassessment. The evidence presented in this book argues against this common assumption, with both social and criminal justice policy implications. Immigration opponents have an adversarial stance against new Latinos, and the consequences of that posture affect older Latinos as well, since most reside in similar communities. Policies designed to combat immigration or punish immigrants are counterproductive, since many have resettled here and are unlikely to return, even if they wanted to.

Therefore I ask: In what ways does immigration reduce levels of criminal violence in Latino communities? What kinds of policies would strengthen the crime-reduction effects of immigration and which might weaken them? Of course, high levels of fear of crime and immigrants, and the extraordinary level of punitive measures in the United States, means that harsh punishment is a routine part of everyday life. Not only does the United States have one of the highest recorded rates of incarceration in the world, in U.S. district courts the prosecution of noncitizens from 1984 to 1994 quadrupled.[34] Two factors give this last finding particular relevance. First, many of these offenses are minor drug-related charges, but a substantial number are immigration offenses (which means Latinos are more susceptible than other ethnic groups and to which native-born Americans are rarely exposed). Second, as we know from figure 3.1, the number of immigrants increased at least four to five times throughout this period, and this growth parallels the prosecution finding. The effects of harsher sentences may prove consequential in the long run if it succeeds in removing large numbers of Latino males from their families, social networks, and communities, and encourages an even tougher opposition to legal status by those seeking documentation.

What about the legal vs. illegal distinctions? Social programs designed to encourage positive messages, such as concrete funding for English-language instruction, instead of negative symbolic measures such as English-only bills, will ultimately help less educated newcomers turn their short-term liabilities into long-term assets.[35] Policy approaches sending a punitive message to immigrant Latinos are less likely to succeed than those educating and encouraging an existing (but poor) labor force to obtain more and better employment. In turn, this means that a population and community with thriving conditions, instead of one residing in the midst of a negative climate singled out by immigration opponents, could provide opportunities for advancement and perhaps develop even more potential to prevent violent crime. A clandestine life, on the other hand, creates more possibility for conflict, and prohibited immigrants are easier to exploit, more likely to offer targets for violent predators, and less likely to report victimization to authorities.[36]

Some policies might even *encourage* Latino crime more than for other ethnic groups. In writing this book it became apparent that distinguishing between "illegal" and "legal" Latinos would be a formidable task. In fact, it was difficult to make that distinction. We saw in chapter 4 that even some of the oldest barrios, many of which existed for almost a hundred years and undoubtedly had even older roots in the community, had substantial numbers of newcomers. I also demonstrated in chapters 2 and 3 that it was difficult to decipher the notion of "legality" in the "immigration" and "Latino studies" literature and to comfortably assess those features in studies of crime. If illegality generates even more illicit activities, disorganizes community life, anchors Latinos into a permanent class of workers who stay poor, and, of course, provides crime-facilitating linkages to the barrio, "illegal" immigration would have to be taken into account. Illegal immigrants would have to be removed, and the supply of new ones stopped. Addressing the "illegal" problem would have to be accepted by community leaders, residents, scholars, and policymakers *if* it would reduce violent crime such as homicide.[37]

There are at least two obstacles discouraging this disruptive and misguided strategy. First and foremost, there was little evidence that immigrants were more crime-prone than native-born Latinos or other citizens. There was even less evidence that "illegal" immigrants were overly involved in violent crime, or at least much more so than "legal" immigrants, at least on San Diego's border. It is also clear that many Latinos, economically speaking, live on the margins of society, and it is hard to imagine urban conditions any worse in the U.S. than those in the border barrios. Singling out those who are "illegal" from those who are not perpetuates the stigmatization of those who are already feared and rejected. This is a heavy price to pay when the evidence on immigrant crime differs from popular impressions—that is, Latino violence is not as harsh as expected given impoverished conditions, but instead is buffered by service sector jobs and work in the informal economy.

Second, "illegal aliens" cannot be thoroughly separated from legal ones. It is difficult to think of a single community in this study where illegal aliens outnumber those who are not, or even a series of street blocks where one could point out and distinguish those with documentation from others. Instead, many are blended into poor Latino families and neighborhoods and should not be deported (even though this occurs), since this tends to break up families as well as weaken social bonds and community cohesion, thereby disrupting local conditions and adversely impacting nonimmigrants. This policy "solution" thereby potentially wreaks more havoc on disadvantaged communities than the deleterious consequences of poor structural conditions. Imagine a family where one parent (or child) has legal documentation, but another doesn't and is deported after residing in the United States for several years. Rather than encouraging a transient and perhaps cross-national life, steps to integrate those without "papers" into legal residence would probably prove less harmful in the long run than the traditional use of deportation. New Latinos are here to stay, and they are embedded in social networks with older ones, rendering the legal vs. illegal distinction untenable.

Nevertheless, even if immigration opponents accept my evidence, some pundits will continue to oppose merging legal and illegal Latinos because of the "job issues" used by many as a tactic to oppose low-wage workers. Some will continue to insist that "illegals" are flooding into this country and taking away good-paying jobs from hardworking Americans. Even if I'm right about the crime issue, there is still the larger economic issue of Latino immigrants working in low-end construction jobs,[38] or other occupations in the meat-packing industry, or picking fruit, or driving taxis—jobs that presumably everyone wants but cannot get, since immigrants are taking them away.

It might be prudent to reiterate that these jobs attract people willing to accept low wages and more dangerous working conditions than U.S.-born workers are. Latino immigrants do not necessarily seek to take jobs from natives, nor do they search for employment with unsafe working conditions and high mortality rates. Regardless of how immigration opponents and proponents respond to the economic and crime issues raised in this book, it is now clear that Latinos are a central topic in the process of defining the role of how and where newcomers fit into American society. A serious contribution to the urban crime problem is not one of them.

FUTURE RESEARCH

For at least a generation, policies designed to address the "poverty problem" have also been popularly perceived as a "race problem."[39] There is no doubt that ethnic minorities are poorer than Whites and that inequality hits the former harder than it does others. However, the identification of ethnic minorities as poor has in turn fueled heated and even distorted policy debates over discrimination, affirmative action, welfare, family disruption, and urban crime.[40] Redefining race and inequality requires that the newcomers be incorporated into a renewed debate and that the issue of its consequences on violence be resolved.

Some of these policies (e.g., welfare) have not generally acknowledged that the origins of poverty vary; that its consequences and perpetuation change; that differences exist between "old" and "new" poverty; and that Latino immigration forces a new look at race, poverty, and, of course, crime.

Like others, I close by stating the obvious: Much more research needs to be conducted on Latinos and crime to advance our knowledge beyond the conclusions drawn in this book. There are several significant issues not captured in my analysis. We need more studies on other forms of violent crime (e.g., stranger robbery, domestic violence) to determine whether these activities vary over time or across contexts of reception and ethnicity. Some Latinos might be at greater risk of robbery in urban areas, while others are involved in domestic violence situations, both possibly due to poor economic status and the stress associated with adaptation to a new life. At some point, Latinos—immigrants and nonimmigrants alike—become Americanized in terms of their criminal involvement. The questions then are at what degree of integration are Latinos engaging in violence like others, and when does that take place? Does assimilation dampen violence? At this stage it is uncertain when or if some Latinos become "superpredators" and others don't, particularly among those exposed to warlike conditions in their home countries but who have managed to reach the United States.

Other crime types demand further exploration—for example, the far more numerous nonfatal and more routine crimes of burglary and theft. Property crimes comprise the vast majority of reported crime in the United States, and evidence of generational and native-born distinctions in this area would substantiate, or refute, claims of crime-prone rather than violence-prone immigrants. Results from those studies would require a look at offending patterns as well as victimization. Taken together, evidence on property and violence crimes would afford a comprehensive examination of Latino crime.

The consequences of criminal activities at various stages of the criminal justice system—arrest, sentencing, and imprisonment—and how those vary by immigration status also warrant attention. Given the size of the young Latino population and its all-but-certain continuing growth in future years, the cumulative disadvantage that results from the manner in which the criminal justice system treats Latinos should be of practical concern. As Steffensmeier and Demeuth[41] put it, "As socially disadvantaged offenders and recent immigrants, Latino defendants may lack the resources (financial, cultural) to resist or soften the imposition of harsh penalties. They also may feel alienated from a system they believe treats them unfairly and hence seem more recalcitrant. Lastly, their offense behavior may be viewed as more threatening. Judges and prosecutors concerned with maintaining order and protecting communities may be influenced, at least subliminally, by widespread attributions connecting Latino males to drug-trafficking networks and drug-related violence. On the basis of these attributions, court officials may project behavioral expectations about the defendant's rehabilitative potential of potential danger to the community."

The danger of disparate treatment for Latino youths is only compounded by the harsh incarceration policies that have captured the imagination of voters. For reasons already discussed, Latinos are more susceptible to border patrol activities, urban police patrols profiling gang members, and harsh treatment in the federal criminal justice system. The consequences of these activities are not hard to discern in the impoverished barrios of San Diego, El Paso, Houston, and Chicago. From a long-term perspective, research in these areas should be strengthened rather than ignored in light of the present evidence that Latinos are not high-rate killers.

Another significant issue that warrants attention concerns the growth and effects of Latinos in rural areas. As seen in earlier chapters, the emphasis on urban crime dynamics represents the most significant example of theory and research on crime and community-level processes because of population size, changes over time, and economic disadvantage.[42] The importance of urbanization is common in the immigration literature; Latinos and violence are concentrated in these areas, and it is understandable that studies focus on ethnic minorities and urban crime.

However, many Latinos are entering small towns of no more than fifty thousand and rural settings of fewer than twenty-five hundred in population.[43] Rural places in North Carolina, Arkansas, Georgia, Tennessee, Nevada, and Iowa have experienced phenomenal Latino growth, and the consequences of this process remain to be seen. For instance, will rural Latinos be more or less assimilated and subject to discrimination than urban Latinos? Will these practices shape criminal victimization, involvement, and criminal justice decision-making processes? There obviously is a need for more criminological research on urban, rural, and, of course, suburban areas that includes Latinos.

Finally, other important issues have not been adequately covered. What happens when first-generation immigrants have locally grown children? After many years of weakened connections, conceptions of poverty "relative to" the old country become less salient, and the impact of the persistence of social ties on criminality could diminish. Will Latino crime then approach those of other ethnic minority groups? Historical research leads us to expect an increase in violence. But will Latino communities again provide an exception to expectations? What about Asian and Afro-Caribbean ethnic group differences vis-à-vis crime? While poor or working poor, will their job attachments explain less, or more, criminal involvement than for Latinos? Will the strength of immigration, again, explain potential ethnic differences?

Although these issues are important to examine in the future, my main findings bear repeating: Structural explanations, including high levels of job attachments and social capital, and relative deprivation explanations, especially lower economic expectations than native-born Americans, largely account for patterns of Latino homicide. This underscores the effects of deprivation but reminds us that the effects should be recast to consider contemporary situations and illustrates the need to include Latinos in future research. There is no doubt that much more research remains to be done in this area and that these suggestions, questions, and findings are the tip of the iceberg.

Yet, by focusing on Latinos and homicide in these five cities, the conclusions presented in this book demonstrate that Latinos are not usually engaged in high levels of violent crime and that immigration can be a positive influence that suppresses crime. Until now, this group has largely gone ignored, and this notion has rarely been explored. But the incorporation of Latinos into criminological research will inevitably intensify, and when it does, my hope is that this book will provide a foundation on which others can build studies that effectively capture meaningful group differences, as well as a rationale for moving beyond Black and White comparisons. Since the United States increasingly resembles its multiethnic cities and since Latino-majority communities are proliferating, the time has come to ask more questions about Latinos and crime.

9. AFTERWORD

WHILE THE LATINO BACKLASH peaked in California toward the end of the 1990s, it ebbed and flowed in different ways in Texas and other states. There was not an end to the singling out of Latinos and immigrants but a subtle acceptance that Latinos were here to stay. Most Americans seemed to come to terms with the fact that stigmatizing an ethnic group inevitably leads to regrouping; reorganizing; and, ultimately, the reappearance of the targeted group as a more active and solidified force. This pattern has been happening for decades. After a period of absorption into mainstream society, immigrant groups organize and seek fuller political participation in America. They have done so in different ways, including lobbying for legislation designed to accommodate newcomers; registering voters; and ousting the most egregious politicians whose careers were built on demonizing ethnic minorities.

The election of 1996 demonstrated this, destroying the national aspirations of nativist California politicians, halting the local rise of others even more divisive, and bringing to the forefront those whose power and prominence were intertwined with Latinos. The growing hostility in the Latino/a community was demonstrated by the Latino and Immigrants' Rights March on October 13, 1996, which reflected the Latino community's anger at the anti-immigrant and anti-Latino sentiment in America. This march was the first mass national protest by Latinos, and a month later, Latino voters, buoyed by registration drives, citizenship campaigns, and get-out-the-vote drives, and angered over the anti-Latino posture, swelled the numbers of Latino voters in California and other places. The sleeping giant had finally risen, and this protest represented the first step to a larger presence on the national scene.

In the post–Proposition 187 era, significant changes seemed to be taking place: political strategists recruited Latinos; candidates spoke Spanish; and at least one border state governor boasted of his closeness to the newly elected president of Mexico in the 2000 election. Al Gore and George W. Bush tried to speak Spanish, and the latter frequently appeared with his bilingual nephew.

For a while it even became chic to be Latino, and the media brought Ricky Martin, Jennifer Lopez, and other Latino and Latina entertainers into America's homes. Many were living and dancing to "La Vida Loca" while watching Latinos and Latinas on television. Meanwhile, the comfort with Latinos merged with a booming economy depending heavily on the backs and sweat of Latino immigrants. That labor provided a boost to America and immigrants alike. Latinos reinvigorated many dying towns and depopulated states that had long denied them access to jobs in their stockyards, chicken farms, and agricultural fields.

Meanwhile, violent crime dropped to levels not seen in at least a generation. The speculation rose as to why and how crime declined— fewer youths, less drug violence, harsher and longer sentences, diminished access to guns and drugs, and a host of other reasons, even some speculation that more immigrants meant less crime, since they were not yet "Americanized" into the realities of urban life. Whatever the reasons, the epidemic of youth violence was stopped and was tipping back to record lows. Latinos were still stigmatized by many in the media, but the national anger had subsided. For some time in 2001 there was even talk from inside the Bush White House of legalizing Mexican workers, making life safe for the undocumented, and bringing justice to many who had fled injustice south of the U.S. border. Of course, this talk was geared more at ensuring Latino/a votes than out of a sense of social justice, but even recognizing the political clout of Latinos/as can be seen as progress.

That all ended in the aftermath of the September 11, 2001, terrorist attacks on the World Trade Center, the Pentagon, and on United Flight 93 in Pennsylvania. Whatever momentum immigrant proponents generated came to a crashing halt. Instead, immigration opponents took advantage of the latest alarm. Concerns about losing control of our borders reappeared in light of the vast destruction, the mass killings, the economic plunge, and the subsequent large layoffs. The new argument was that new workers might not be needed after all. In the end, a handful of Islamic fundamentalists halted the Latino—that is, immigrant—movement and brought it back in some ways to the 1980 starting point; immigrants were again stigmatized and stereotyped.

Even with the latest setback, however, both new and old Latinos will become increasingly influential as America once again waits to decide yet again: Are we welcoming newcomers or turning them away?

GLOSSARY

ARROZ CON POLLO. A chicken-and-rice dish that is popular in many Latino areas.

BALSERO. Slang used to describe Cuban entering the United States illegally on a boat or a boat-raft.

BARRIO. Community, neighborhood, or enclave dominated by Latinos.

BODEGAS. In heavily Dominican or Puerto Rican neighborhoods refers to corner stores. Term is also used to describe packing sheds along the Mexican border.

BORICUAN. Nickname for Puerto Rican.

BRACERO. Generally used to describe Mexican guest worker. Typically works in agricultural fields along the Mexican border.

CAFÉ CON LECHE. Steamed milk and espresso drink popular in Cuban storefronts in Miami.

CALIFORNIO. A native Californian of Mexican origin.

CALLE OCHO. Nickname for Eighth Street or Tamiami Trail in Miami.

CAMINO REAL. Spanish trail in colonial Mexico. Connected Mexico to far reaches of contemporary United States.

CANTINA. Neighborhood bar.

CERVEZA. Beer.

CHICANO. Slang for person of Mexican origin.

COLONIA. Originally used to describe rural Mexican communities. Now also refers to unincorporated and margalized communities along Texas/Mexican border.

CONQUISTADORE. Spanish conqueror.

EL NORTE. Term used by Latino immigrants to describe North America or north of the Mexican border.

EL OTRO LADO. Slang for "The other side," or the United States.

EL PASO DEL RIO DEL NORTE. Original name for El Paso, Texas, coined by Spanish settlers in colonial Mexico.

GALAVISION. A major Spanish-speaking television network viewed in many U.S. Latino households.

INCAN. Person descended from the Inca Empire in Central America.
INDIO. Slang for person with indigenous features.

JEFE. A boss or chief.

MARIELITO. Slang for Cuban who arrived in the United States through the port of Mariel in the 1980 boatlift.
MAYAN. Person descended from the Maya Empire in Central America.
MEJICANO. A person from Mexico.
MERENGUE. Fast-paced music originally from the Dominican Republic.
MESTIZO. Offspring of Spanish and Indian or indigenous blood.
MOTA. Border slang for marijuana.
MULATO. Offspring of Spanish and African blood.

NORTENO. Music from the northern Mexican frontier. Sometimes refers to as "frontera" sound.

PACHUCO. Slang for street tough.
PATRONES. Double connotation. Political bosses or benefactors.
PLATANOS. Green bananas used in Caribbean cuisine.

SALSA. Music from the Caribbean mixed with New York City sounds. Also refers to a spicy sauce.

TEJANO. A native Texan of Mexican origin.

NOTES

INTRODUCTION

1. See, for example, Suro 1998 and Montejano 1999.
2. See Schmitt 2001. The 1980 population figures are taken from Bean and Tienda 1987.
3. Quoted in Schmitt 2001.
4. According to David Montejano in the introduction to his edited book *Chicano Politics and Society in the Late Twentieth Century,* racial tension and anxiety about the consequences of immigration motivated many of the reactions described in this introduction, as Latinos became the fastest-growing segment of the American population. He notes that "the browning of America" has become a popular topic in a contemporary public discourse that is fraught with concern about another ethnic divide, one that moves beyond the traditional Black and White dichotomy that has long framed our conceptions of race (Montejano 1999).
5. The emergence of this ethnic minority group has also been highlighted by a number of visible and violent events since 1980. These include three major riots in Miami throughout the 1980s sparked largely by the actions of Latino police officers and hostility toward Latino newcomers; a spring 1991 disturbance in a Washington, D.C., immigrant Latino community over aggressive police tactics; and the 1992 Los Angeles riots, which resulted in the arrest of many immigrant Latino looters. Other incidents include the videotaped police beating of "illegal aliens" in Riverside, California; the recent U.S. Marine killing of a Chicano citizen while patrolling the Mexican border outside of Presidio, Texas; and the widely publicized murder of Tejano singer Selena Quintanilla.
6. See Zucker and Zucker 1996: 62–63.
7. For an account of the border issue see Nevins 2002. Chapter 1 in Nevins provides critical commentary on this argument.
8. Highlighted in Gutierrez 1995: 2.
9. See, again, the introductory chapter by Montejano 1999.
10. See chapter 7 for more on the continued perpetuation of this stereotype. The Nevins 2002 account of the creation of border crime and the latest "Mexican scare" in the San Diego region was influential in shaping this section.
11. See Brimelow 1995: 182 for egregious claims on immigrants and crime; Mann 1996 provides counter.

12. See Mann 1996: 38, table 2-1.

13. For more on the centrality of Latino rates see Wilbanks 1984; Martinez and Lee 1999b. See also Roger Lane 1986: 4 for similar comment on Latino and Asian rates.

14. Margaret Zahn (1987) provides an original explanation for Latinos built on previous work distinguishing between relative and absolute deprivation. She emphasizes the need to examine new and older arrivals when examining the poverty and Latino homicide connection. I elaborate on the Zahn argument in chapter 3.

15. At times I use "Black" as a global label. When appropriate and possible I distinguish "African Americans" from "Afro Caribbeans" in the text and tables. A large foreign-born Black population, heavily Haitian, exists in the city of Miami but not in the other four cities investigated in this book.

16. Exploring homicide or any other type of violent crime in any detail, in New York City or Los Angeles alone, would have been a daunting undertaking, even with the advances in computer technology that were not available when this project started. I did, however, write to Chief Bernard C. Parks of the Los Angeles Police Department, seeking access to homicide unit entries, which apparently "are scattered throughout eighteen different geographic areas, making citywide searching and retrieval cumbersome and difficult," and access was eventually declined (personal communication). New York City has dozens of precincts and homicide units, making this an even more difficult task to perform. Jeffrey Fagan has collected and coded homicide data for a sample of young males, but this project will require more time and effort to complete, due to decentralized storage, logistics difficulties, and the sheer number of cases.

17. See Portes and Rumbaut 1996 for background on immigration trends and the recent immigrant experience.

18. See Moore and Pinderhughes 1993 for collective work by themselves and others on Latinos and city and neighborhood changes in nine cities or areas.

19. See Russell 1998 for fear of crime and racial hoaxes.

20. Again, Brimelow 1995 and Montejano 1999 offer differing perspectives.

21. See Escobar 1999 for a historical viewpoint and seminal work on the relationship between Chicanos and the police in Los Angeles.

22. The voluminous publication by the National Research Council Panel on the Understanding and Control of Violent Behavior is but one example of the inattention to Latino homicide (Reiss and Roth 1993). Data presented in several graphs focus on Black or White homicide rates, and a few incorporate Asian and Native American data. I do not want to suggest that the authors purposely ignored Latinos, and I know that national data are difficult to obtain on Latinos. At the same time, data presented never directly examine Latinos in any figures, and Latinos are rarely mentioned in the text.

23. See Brimelow 1995; Kennedy 1996; and Miles 1992 for examples of popular writings promoting the latest panic over Mexicans and immigrants. But, again, see Montejano 1999 for critical comments on these writings. Nevins (2002: 172) provides further context for the latest stereotypical threat. This is highlighted and discussed in chapter 7.

24. As best as I can determine, long-term and reliable data for Latino criminal homicide, offender rates, or motivating circumstances are nonexistent. According to current FBI agent and former statistician at the FBI's Uniform Crime Reports (UCR) Rick Florence, a policy board of police chiefs suggested mandatory collection of "Hispanic ethnicity" for the UCR's 1980 supplemental homicide reports. At that time many police agencies were in locales with few Latinos, and, after 1980, collection of "Hispanic" ethnicity variables was made voluntary. As a result, most agencies dropped the Hispanic designation, many Latinos are recorded as White or in another racial category, and use of the ethnicity variables differs (personal communication, June 1996). Still, use of the "Hispanic origin" variable differs across time and jurisdiction, but even today it is not completely recorded.

25. See LaFree 1998 for an example.

26. Rumbaut 1995 provides data on immigrant Latinos. See also Martinez and Lee 2000 for association between immigration and crime changes.

27. Jacqueline Cohen and colleagues 1998 concisely describe this interaction; see also Miller 1996 for insightful writing on the causes and consequences of the crack-cocaine epidemic.

28. For popular writings on this topic and on Latinos see Beck 1996; Tanton and Lutton 1993. These polemics are based largely on quotes, anecdotes, personal impressions, or reviews of works by social scientists.

29. According to Portes 1996; Vigil 1980; and Waters 1999 there will be generation differences in levels of criminal activity. As the children of immigrants become more "Americanized" and socialized into mainstream society, the second generation will become more crime-prone than new immigrants.

30. It is interesting to note that the post–World War II record high national murder rate of 10.2 in 1980 preceded the latest immigration wave.

31. Suro 1998: 319.

32. Montejano 1999; Santoro 1999.

33. Again, see Nevins (2002) for convincing commentary on the origins of Operation Gatekeeper in the San Diego region. This INS initiative was designed to deter Mexican nationals from crossing the border.

34. American Friends Service Committee 1999; Eschbach et al. 1999; see Webb 1957 for more on this "old problem" that periodically resurfaces.

35. Bureau of the Census 1995; Escobar 1999; Lollock 2001.

36. I use "barrio" and "enclave" to describe heavily Latino neighborhoods. In tra-

ditional usage "barrio" is a distinctly Mexican community. Many barrios originated as Mexican "colonias" or colonies in the 1800s and originally were the
center of town or plazas in the Southwest. American growth passed these
areas, and they eventually grew more isolated from the rest of the city (Moore
and Pachon 1985). Basically, "enclave" originally describes a labor market
based on immigrant human capital in Miami's Cuban community and focused
on entrepreneurs. But now some refer to Cuban-dominant areas in metropolitan Miami as enclaves (Portes and Bach 1985).

37. See Shaw and McKay 1931 and 1969 for the legacy on the effects of immigra-
    tion in Chicago neighborhoods that led to later work in American sociology.
38. See chapter 2 for a brief overview of Latino identity.
39. Velez-Ibañez 1993 describes Latinos and the working poor.
40. See the introduction in Moore and Pinderhughes 1993.
41. According to William J. Wilson 1987 and 1996, extreme disadvantage or
    extremely high levels of poverty, consequences of deindustrialization, hit urban
    ethnic minorities more than other ethnic groups in the 1970s and 1980s.
42. See Moore and Pinderhughes 1993.
43. Bean and Tienda 1987.
44. See Rumbaut 1995.
45. Rumbaut 1995: 6.
46. See Betancur 1996 for a description of Mexican and Puerto Rican movement
    into Chicago.
47. See Carolyn Rebecca Block, Richard L. Block, and the Illinois Criminal Justice
    Information Authority, *Homicides in Chicago, 1965–1995* [computer file],. 4th
    ICPSR version. Chicago: Illinois Criminal Justice Information Authority [pro-
    ducer], 1998. Ann Arbor, Mich.: MI: Interuniversity Consortium for Political
    and Social Research [distributor], 1998.
48. Lane 1997 describes historical use of homicide data.
49. See LaFree 1998.
50. LaFree 1998: 17–19.
51. Short 1997: 25.
52. Ousey 1999: 410.
53. Merton 1938 provided the intellectual foundation for this type of research.
54. See Gonzalez 2000 for panoramic writing on Latino history in the United
    States.

THE LEGACY AND IMAGES OF LATINO CRIME

1. See Woll 1987: 171–73; Vigil 1998: 155–59 provides a historical account of
   these images.
2. Again, Woll 1987 provides more on this genre.

3. Woll 1987.
4. See Clara Rodriguez 1997.
5. Quoted in Martinez and Lee 2000b: 488.
6. Martinez and Lee 2000b.
7. Escobar 1999: 8.
8. Martinez and Lee 2000b.
9. Shaw and McKay 1969 (1942).
10. See also Sampson and Lauritsen 1997.
11. Yeager 1997.
12. See Taft 1936 and Gurr 1989.
13. See Alaniz, Cartmill, and Parker 1998 for alcohol outlet and serious crime connection in three California cities.
14. Short 1997: 6–10.
15. Thrasher 1927: 57.
16. Short 1997: 80.
17. Escobar 1999: 9–12.
18. See chapter 8 in Vigil 1998. As one example, an LAPD police chief describes how "It seems just, however, to say that Mexicans are unmoral rather than immoral since they lack a conception of morals as understood in this country. Their housing conditions are bad, crime is prevalent and their morals are a menace to our civilization. They are illiterate, ignorant and inefficient and have few firm religious beliefs" (quoted in Vigil 1998: 225). Such a perception would hardly seem supportable given the low rate of Latino homicides.
19. As cited in McWilliams 1968 (1949): 233–234. Escobar 1999: 211–13 argues that the Ayres report reflected a common sentiment among the Los Angeles law-enforcement community and was widely echoed by others in that time period. One consequence was that police would treat Mexican youths harsher and with more punitive measures than most other youths.
20. McWilliams 1968 (1949): 235.
21. Escobar 1999: 11.
22. Gans 1992: 173–74.
23. See Lane 1997.
24. Cf. Wilson 1987; Anderson 1990.
25. Bankston 1998; see also Vigil and Long 1990.
26. See Sanchez-Jankowski 1991.
27. Lewis 1965.
28. Wolfgang and Ferracuti 1967; see also Anderson 1999.
29. Wolfgang 1958: 188–89.
30. Sampson and Lauritsen 1997.
31. Sutherland 1947.
32. Sellin 1938.

33. Sutherland and Cressey 1960.
34. Lind 1930.
35. Padilla 1980.
36. Sellin 1938: 85.
37. Bankston 1998; see Moore 1993: 83–85 for a similar argument about Chicanos. As Mexican-American youths became more Americanized or were several generations old they were more likely to join gangs and engage in serious offenses.
38. Chin 1990; Du Phuoc Long 1996.
39. Portes 1996: 3.
40. Bursik 1988: 521.
41. Bankston 1998.
42. See Thomas and Znaniecki (1918 and 1920).
43. Thomas and Znaniecki 1920: 2.
44. Thomas and Znaniecki 1920.
45. Thomas and Znaniecki 1984: 286.
46. See Shaw and McKay 1931, 1969. See also Ross 1937; Kobrin 1959.
47. Shaw and McKay 1969: 158.
48. Jonassen 1949: 613.
49. Sampson and Lauritsen 1997.
50. Sampson and Lauritsen 1997: 340; see also Sampson and Wilson 1995.
51. Again, see Sampson and Lauritsen 1997: 340.
52. Portes and Rumbaut 1993.
53. Brimelow 1995.
54. Hagan and Palloni 1998.
55. See Lane 1997: 298.
56. Gurr 1989; Monkkonen 1989.
57. Young 1936.
58. Handlin 1959.
59. Abbott 1915; Lind 1930; Taft 1936; Hagan and Palloni 1998; Tonry 1997; Ferracuti 1968; Sellin 1938.
60. Tonry 1997: 21.
61. Again, see Tonry 1997: 21.
62. McCord 1995.
63. For example, immigrants in Boston, but not Chicago, were disproportionately involved in crime.
64. Hagan and Palloni 1998; Sellin 1938; Sutherland 1934.
65. Although lower than native Blacks, see Bowler 1931: 119.
66. Taylor 1931: 235.
67. Escobar 1999: 186–90.
68. Taylor 1932: 143.

69. Lane 1997; Wolfgang 1958.
70. See McKanna 1997 for more on ethnic minorities in the frontier West.
71. Hagan and Palloni 1998 explore this issues on the border.
72. Again, European immigrants such as Italians and Irish (Lane 1997).
73. Martinez and Lee 1999 examine Miami.
74. Bradshaw, Johnson, Cheatwood, and Blanchard 1998 provide evidence, but in San Antonio.
75. Bullock 1955 was one of the first to explore this issue.
76. Pokorny 1965 again uses Houston as a research site.
77. See Beasley and Antunes 1974 and Mladenka and Hill 1976 for more on findings from Houston data.
78. See Martinez and Lee 1999 for a review of this literature.
79. Betancur 1996 describes Latino Chicago.
80. One of the first explorations of Latino homicide in Chicago and comparisons to Whites and Blacks is in Block 1985.
81. Alaniz, Cartmill, and Parker 1998 control for the fraction of the population that is immigrant in three cities and find not significant findings.
82. Rosenwaike and Hempstead 1990 look at Puerto Ricans in various areas.
83. Wilbanks 1984.
84. Bean and Tienda 1987.
85. See Portes and Stepick 1993 for background.
86. See Martinez and Lee 1999 for further information.
87. Martinez 1997a.
88. Martinez 1997b.
89. Martinez and Lee 1998.
90. Lee, Martinez, and Rodriguez 2000 provide Latino contrast in Miami and El Paso. Although different in terms of regional location, both cities are predominantly Latino.
91. See Martinez 1996 for a discussion of absolute verses relative deprivation among Latinos.
92. Wilbanks 1984; see also Epstein and Greene 1993.
93. See Hawkins 1999 for a similar disaggregation strategy.
94. Martinez and Lee (2000a) were among the first to compare and contrast foreign-born Black homicide circumstances. While Mariel Cubans are not all of Afro origin, many were, and this ethnic group is retained as a comparison point.
95. See also Portes and Stepick 1993.
96. See Short 1997.
97. The Latino violence literature is a relevant topic, such as ethnographies about Latino gangs, but the etiology of serious Latino violence is similar to the etiology of Latino homicide

98. Zahn 1987: 13–30.
99. Mercy 1987: 1–12.
100. Spence 1987: 135–50.
101. Again, Latino homicide rates fall somewhere between those of Blacks and Whites, even in areas where Latinos are different—that is, usually Mexican in one place and Puerto Rican in another.
102. Valdez and Nourjah 1987: 85–100.
103. Leyba 1987: 101–18.

THE CREATION OF LATINOS

1. See Gonzalez 2000: xiii.
2. The popular backlash was remarkably swift and reflected the contentiousness of this debate (Gutierrez 1995). Consider the 1994 passage of Proposition 187 in California, recent English-only legislation in many states, continued efforts to end bilingual education, concerted attempts to stem the flow of Cuban refugees with wet-foot/dry-foot policy. Cubans caught at sea are returned to Cuba, but those who land are released into the community.
3. See Gonzalez's introduction in *A History of Latinos in America*.
4. Again, see Gonzalez (2000) and Nevins (2002) for more on the extent of the Latino backlash in California.
5. Gonzalez 2000; Suro 1998.
6. Camarillo 1981; Martinez 1979; and Montejano 1984 all provide background on the origins of California and Texas communities.
7. Taylor 1932; Gutierrez 1995.
8. Gonzalez 2000.
9. Padilla 1947 provides one of the first accounts of Puerto Ricans in Chicago.
10. As best as I can determine, Pedraza (1997) is one of the first to distinguish among Cubans, especially Marielitos and Balseros.
11. Again, see Nevins 2002.
12. See Zucker and Zucker 1996: 62.
13. See the works Fox 1996; Massey 1993; Montejano 1999; and Skerry 1993.
14. Rodolfo de la Garza (1993) discusses these issues and topics in more detail.
15. See Moore and Pinderhughes 1993. But Oboler (1995) describes Latino identity in more detail.
16. Aguirre and Saenz 1991; see also Moore and Pinderhughes 1993; Oboler 1995.
17. In general I use "Latino" as a generic term describing the Latino population, regardless of gender, to avoid redundancy or usage of "Latino/a." When making necessary gender distinctions I will refer specifically to "Latinas" as female Latinos, and talk about "Latino males" to delineate gender descriptions.

18. Fox 1993.
19. De la Garza et al. 1993.
20. See again De la Garza 1993: 13.
21. With rare exceptions homicide data are not coded in this manner. Most of the files I worked with used generic codes of "Hispanic" or "Latino" regularly.
22. De la Garza et al. 1993.
23. See Vigil 1998: 104–6.
24. Ibid.
25. Aguirre and Saenz 1991.
26. Massey 1993.
27. Betancur 1996; Oboler 1995.
28. See Oboler 1995.
29. Betancur 1996.
30. Ibid.
31. Massey 1993.
32. Miles 1992; Montejano 1999.
33. Camarota 1998 provides more on the intergroup-conflict argument.
34. De la Garza 1993.
35. Moore and Pinderhughes 1993.
36. Aguirre and Saenz 1991.
37. Short 1997.
38. Portes 1987.
39. Aguirre and Saenz 1991.
40. Suro 1998.
41. Suro 1998: 6–8.
42. Rumbaut 1995.
43. Ibid.
44. Holmes 1996.
45. Other Central American groups in Houston exist, especially indigenous Incans and Mayans. For more on this topic see Hagan 1994.
46. Suro 1998.
47. See Rumbaut 1995: 2.
48. Data sources on Latino nonlethal violence exist. Some National Crime Victimization Survey (NCVS) results on Latino personal crimes are available, but the race/ethnic categories are nationally aggregated data and not mutually exclusive. To illustrate, a Latino victim could count as "White" and "Latino," and the residual category of "non-Latino" consists of both "White and "Black" respondents. In spite of these severe shortcomings—which highlight a basic issue motivating the proposed research—the results indicate that Latinos have higher personal victimization rates than the total population, but the rates also vary by type of personal crime. Latino robbery victimization closely resembles that of

Blacks. In other crimes, the Latino victimization rate falls between the White and the Black rates, and for rape is slightly lower than the national average.

49. Council of Economic Advisers 1999. See http://w3.access.gpo.gov/eop/ca/index.html.
50. The Latino homicide rate is the number of Latino homicides per 100,000 Latinos.
51. Shaw and McKay 1931; 1969.
52. Muller 1993; cf. Pennell et al. 1989.
53. Brimelow 1995; for counter see Gutierrez 1995.
54. Gonzalez 2000.
55. Brimelow 1995.
56. Scalia 1996 provides data on noncitizen imprisonment.
57. See Gonzalez 2000: 194–95 for critique.
58. See Lamm 1984: 49.
59. Gonzalez 2000: 195.
60. Ibid.
61. See Beck 1996; Hagan and Palloni 199; Short 1997.
62. Simon 1987; Portes and Stepick 1993; Roper Reports 1982, 1992, 1995. See exhibit 2 in Martinez and Lee 2000b: 508.
63. Roper Reports 1995.
64. Beck 1996. I discuss this in more detail in chapter 6.
65. See Nevins 2002; Suro 1998.
66. Juan Gonzalez 2000: 196.
67. Brimelow 1995.
68. American Friends Service Committee 2000 describes many of these incidents in detail.
69. See again American Friends Service Committee 2000.
70. See http://www.afsc.org/border00.htm for information on these cases.
71. Blumstein 1995; Cook and Laub 1999.
72. DiIulio, Bennett, and Walters 1996; see also Wilson 1992.
73. See Zatz and Mann 1998: 1–12.
74. Portillos 1998: 156–66; Rodriguez 1998: 130–33.
75. For a similar situation in the "zoot suit" era discussed in chapter 4 see Escobar 1999.
76. See Nelsen et al. 1994.

THE ORIGINS OF LATINO COMMUNITIES

1. This is not to suggest that Latino immigrants are well off but, that exposure to crime and engaging in criminal activity are less than expected, given impover-

ished conditions. For more on the consequences of European immigration and southern Black migration, see Shaw and McKay 1931.

2. See Sanchez 1993: 129.
3. Garcia 1996: 231; Sanchez 1993: 4–14.
4. Shaw and McKay 1931; 1969: 69.
5. Sampson and Wilson 1995: 42; Short 1997: 48–50.
6. Short 1997: 10.
7. Short (1997) and Sampson and Wilson (1995) point out that differences in urban conditions make Black and White comparisons in U.S. cities difficult if not impossible to carry out. Whites do not live in areas with the same level of poverty as Blacks. Sampson and Wilson (1995: 42) argue that even the worst-case scenario for Whites in terms of level of poverty is far superior to conditions in a typical Black community. Much of this argument is originally drawn from Shaw and McKay 1942: 614–17.
8. See Massey and Denton 1989.
9. Lieberson 1980: 19–41.
10. See Lieberson 1980 for European immigrant context; Montejano 1987 illustrates the southern Texas context, and Sanchez provides the Los Angeles counterpart.
11. Sanchez 1993: 4–5. This body of literature focuses on the adjustment in urban America drawing in part on the work of Handlin 1954. Sanchez provides a detailed overview of the classic works on cultural adaptation and the contradictions facing Latinos in becoming American (1993: 4–10).
12. Montejano 1987.
13. Lieberson 1980.
14. See Montejano 1987: 201.
15. See Gutierrez 1995: 54.
16. Camarillo 1979; Montejano 1987.
17. Martinez 1994.
18. For discussion on evolvement from *municipios* to *barrios* see Camarillo 1979; see also Montejano 1987 for detailed historical context.
19. Garcia 1981; Taylor 1932, 1934.
20. See also Camarillo 1981 for the specific transformation in San Diego and Southern California.
21. Garcia 1981; Camarillo 1981.
22. Herzog 1990 provides historical perspective on the growth of San Diego.
23. Again, Herzog 1990 provides the foundation for much of the description of Logan Heights and Otay Mesa.
24. Herzog 1990.
25. Ibid.

26. Gutierrez 1995: 33–34.
27. See Garcia 1981. Roger Lane describes similar circumstances among African Americans in turn-of-the-twentieth-century Philadelphia (1997: 186–88). The latter borrows heavily from Du Bois (1899), and Lane uses some of Du Bois's work as the foundation for several studies on race and crime in Philadelphia. Lane deserves some credit, especially in his early work (1986) for reintroducing Du Bois to a new generation of scholars during a period when his contributions to early sociological work was overlooked.
28. Gutierrez 1995: 34.
29. Garcia 1981.
30. Romo (1983) notes that this was certainly the case in Los Angeles and probably held true in cities near or close to the border.
31. Rodriguez 1993.
32. See Montejano 1987 for background on systematic harassment of Mexican settlers in colonial Texas.
33. Taken from Rodriguez 1993: 103–5.
34. Rodriguez 1993.
35. The latter also officially known as Little Village.
36. See Betancur 1996; Padilla 1987, 1993.
37. Shaw and McKay 1931; Taylor 1932; Thomas and Znaniecki 1918–20.
38. Again, Betancur 1996 correctly points out many similarities in Mexican and Puerto Rican movement into Chicago.
39. Betancur 1996; see also Taylor 1932 for early perspective on Mexican settlement.
40. Again, see Taylor 1932. Taylor consistently pointed out throughout his career that Mexicans were very different from European immigrants. Unlike others, he consistently collected data to make his argument.
41. Padilla 1993; see also Chicago Historical Society Web site: *www.chicagohs.org/Neighborhoods*. My creation of Chicago neighborhoods borrows heavily from these maps.
42. Taylor 1932; Shaw and McKay 1969.
43. Betancur 1996.
44. Ibid.
45. Betancur 1996: 1302; see Clara Rodriguez 1989 for more on the unique U.S. and Puerto Rico relationship.
46. See Padilla 1947. This is probably one of the earliest works on Puerto Rican Chicago.
47. Padilla 1993: 131.
48. For contemporary reading on these neighborhoods see the firsthand account of Sanchez 2000.
49. This is demonstrated in the next chapter.

50. Again, for more on Puerto Rican Chicago, see Padilla 1987. Clara Rodriguez 1989 provides a critical account of Puerto Rican settlement throughout the United States.
51. Portes and Stepick 1993.
52. For more discussion on the initial wave of Cuban exiles see Pedraza 1996: 262–66. Pedraza characterizes them as the "Elite" of Cuban society.
53. Pedraza 1985, 1996; see also Grenier and Perez 1996; Portes 1987.
54. Garcia 1996.
55. Ibid.; Pedraza-Bailey 1985.
56. Ibid.
57. See Pedraza-Bailey 1985; Portes and Stepick 1993 for details on accommodation and adjustment of the initial wave of Cuban refugees.
58. Garcia 1996.
59. As cited in Garcia 1996: 86.
60. Portes and Stepick 1993.
61. Rumbaut 1995.
62. Sanchez 1993: 70.
63. See also Camarillo 1979; Sanchez 1993: 70; Gutierrez 1995: 57.
64. Which historically has been predominantly Latino. See Martinez 1975; 1994 for more on the "troublesome border."
65. U.S. Bureau of the Census 1990.
66. Pedraza 1996.
67. Grenier and Perez 1996.
68. These are heavily indigenous Mayans and Incans.
69. See Hagan 1994 on Central Americans.
70. Again, see Pedraza-Bailey 1985.
71. Based on research by the author. The table that follows represents the percent of residents that are living below the 1990 poverty level in each city with each respective community listed below the city poverty rate. Some neighborhood names are abbreviated.

Chicago	24	El Paso	26	Houston	22	Miami	33	San Diego	13
L. Square	26	S. Central	71	Magnolia	33	Allapattah	36	Barrio Logan	44
H. Park	34	Central	36	Segundo	41	Wynwood	34	Downtown	23
West Town	32	Northeast	16	Southwest	17	L. Havana	24	San Ysidro	29
Pilsen	26	L. Valley	35	Northwest	22	L. Quarter	40	Otay Mesa	13

72. Betancur 1996: 1305.
73. Northeast El Paso, Southwest and Northwest Houston.
74. For boundaries related to the twenty Latino communities, the author consulted a variety of sources. In the case of Houston I relied primarily on Rodriguez 1993: 102 but also consulted maps published by the City of Houston

Planning and Development Department (http://www.ci.houston.tx.us/departme/planning/map.htm). For Chicago I looked at Padilla 1993: 130 and maps provided by the Chicago Area Geographic Information Study laboratory. For more on the neighborhood boundaries see http://www.cagis.uic.edu/demographics/demographics_intro.html. In constructing San Diego neighborhood boundaries I used maps given to me by homicide investigators. These maps were originally constructed by the SDPD Crime Analysis Unit on March 8, 1999, and outline the eight major divisions in the city. Each division contains several neighborhoods. I took a similar approach in the city of Miami and checked maps of the Miami Police Department Neighborhood Enhancement Team (NET) Areas before constructing the community outlines used in this chapter. I also relied on colleagues' observations, history books, city maps, visitor guides, and newspaper articles on El Paso when compiling those borders.

Once the neigborhood outlines were determined, the next step consisted of aggregating census tracts to fit community profiles. These were not always perfect. Still, they were as close as possible to the community contours. For those interested in reconstructing these files, I have included the city, neighborhood names, and respective census tract number.

Chicago: Logan Square, 2201 through 2229; Humboldt Park, 2301 through 2318; West Town, 2401 through 2436; Pilsen,. 3001 through 3013 and 3101 through 3115.

Houston: Magnolia, 30102, 30901, 30902, 30903, 310, 311; Segundo Barrio, 30022, 30023, 30101, 30200, 30300; Southwest, 41601, 41602, 41603, 41604, 41801, 41904, 41905, 41906, 42501, 42502, 42503, 42504, 42602, 42601, 42701, 42798, 42801, 429, 43301, 42802, 43002, 43002, 431, 43298, 43401, 43402, 43302, 43998; Northwest, 44201, 44202, 44203, 44204, 44301, 44302, 44303, 44304, 44305, 44306, 4401, 4402, 4403, 44401, 44402, 44404, 52800.

San Diego: Otay Mesa, 10004, 10007, 10002, 10003; San Ysidro, 10009, 10008, 10005, 10106, 10109; Downtown, 52, 46, 45, 41, 44, 53, 54. Barrio Logan, 50, 51, 49, 39, 47, 48, 40.

El Paso: South Central/Segundo Barrio, 1800, 1900, 2000, 2100; Central, 22, 23, 24, 25, 26, 27, 28, 33; Lower Valley, 30, 31, 38, 3701, 3702, 3801, 3802, 3902, 4002, 3903, 3901, 3500, 4104, 4001, 4202, 4201, 4105, 4109, 4107, 4103; Northeast, 101, 102, 104, 106, 107, 108, 201, 203, 204.

Miami: Latin Quarter, 5201, 5202, 5301, 53, 3602, 6602; Little Havana, 5001, 5002, 5501, 5502, 6301, 5100, 5401, 5402; Allapattah, 2401, 2402, 25, 29, 3002, 3001; Wynwood 26, 28, 2702.

75. See Dunn 1997.
76. Betancur 1996.
77. On the origins, see Patricios 1994.

78. Shaw and McKay 1931.
79. Escobar 1999.
80. Garcia 1996; Portes and Stepick 1993.

The Roots of Homicide in the Barrio and Enclave

1. All names have been disguised throughout this chapter.
2. The author viewed the investigation of these cases up close and in most instances firsthand. Other than being at the scene of the killing as it occurred, it is difficult to imagine how much closer he could have observed the events themselves.
3. Wilson 1987 and 1996.
4. See the Moore and Pinderhughes introduction to their 1993 edited volume.
5. Gutierrez 1995: 123.
6. For general discussion of the zoot suiters see Mazon 1984.
7. Escobar 1999: 10.
8. As cited by Gutierrez 1995: 125.
9. Gutierrez 1995: 208.
10. Ibid.: 212.
11. For historical roots of these barrios see Garcia 1981.
12. The police arrived, took statements, and the patrons left and went to nearby bars, where the event was reenacted for fellow onlookers over the weekend.
13. See, for example, Martinez, Lee and Nielsen 2001. Contrary to popular expectations, ethnicity and immigration status rarely play a role in the types of homicide involvement of victims or violators. Incident characteristics, such as multiple offenders, or gender and age, were consistently more important influences in shaping homicide circumstances.
14. See Parker 1995 for more on alcohol and homicide.
15. See Thomas and Znaniecki 1918–20.
16. Brimelow 1995; Kennedy 1996; Miles 1992.
17. See Portillos 1998; Mata 1998.
18. Castro 1998: 139.
19. See Sanders 1993 for a similar argument.
20. Sanders 1993.
21. Sanders 1993: 39.
22. Homicide is a rare crime, and most of these homicide motivations are even rarer. These figures provide homicide motivation percentages, since rates are potentially misleading figures. Most are widely skewed and influenced by an extremely small number of cases and population size, which in turn fluctuate by year and neighborhood. I decided to show their presence by providing the overall percentages in which they occurred. This gives a stronger sense of the

frequency of these events and allows us to answer the question at hand: Is a given type of homicide more dominant than others?

23. San Diego Police Department homicide files 1980–95.

24. See also Sanders 1993: 86 for narratives describing similar circumstances.

25. Again, Sanders 1993; see table 4.2 for overall view of local conditions and violence.

26. See Jackall 1997: 65–73 for the penetrating influence of drug trafficking and the corresponding rise in violence. According to Jackall, "Washington Heights has long been the hub of the New York City cocaine trade, with Dominican dealers retailing coke imported wholesale by Cali-cartel Columbians based in Jackson Heights, Queens. In 1985 Washington Heights gave the world crack, a combination of cocaine, baking soda, and various additives such as Bacardi rum, to provide flavor or extra kick, baked together into rocklike form and smoked in glass pipes" (Jackall 1997: 64).

27. See Sanchez 2000 for a local description of gang violence and Latino communities.

28. This is the author's pseudonym. See also Sanchez 2000: 212.

29. Anderson 1999.

30. See the previous chapter.

31. Wilbanks 1984; Wolfgang 1958.

32. By this I mean comprised the majority of all homicides.

33. See Suro 1998.

34. Gutierrez 1995: 212.

THE ETHNIC AND IMMIGRANT HOMICIDE CONTRAST, 1980–95

1. Short 1997: 7.

2. Ibid.: 6.

3. See LaFree 1998; Short 1997.

4. See Short 1997.

5. *Council of Economic Advisers for the President's Initiative on Race,* chapter 7, figure 1, 1998.

6. Some could still say that although I compare Latinos and African Americans on a couple of structural characteristics earlier in the book, there are other characteristics beyond poverty related to stability, various components of economic deprivation, or aspects of single-parent families that are left out, and that were all the relevant characteristics taken into account, the groups of homicide rates would be comparable. To a certain extent this argument is correct. Latino male joblessness is not as high as African-American male joblessness, or following William J. Wilson's argument in *When Work Disappears,*

there are crucial threshold effects (e.g., 40 percent unemployment rates), and that African-American and Latino communities probably differ in the number beyond that threshold (Wilson 1996). The difference, I contend, is that Latino immigration buffers these effects, which otherwise might rise in Latino populations and communications. It is also worth noting that at the very least, *the meaning of poverty* could also vary by ethnic groups and deserves elaboration. I turn to this in the last chapter.

7. See Rodriguez 1993.
8. Martinez 1997; Martinez, Lee, and Nielsen 2001; Martinez and Lee 2000a.
9. For example, armed robbery and aggravated assault.
10. See Lamm and Imhoff 1984.
11. See Martinez 1997; Martinez, Lee, and Nielsen 2001.
12. Lane 1997: 188.
13. Ibid.: 188.
14. See Portillos 1998.
15. Lamm and Imhoff 1984: 30.
16. See Martinez and Lee 2000a.
17. See Du Bois 1899; Monkkonen 2001.
18. This is the percent of a census tract population that arrived between 1980 and 1990.
19. Lee, Martinez, and Rosenfeld 2001.
20. Martinez and Lee 2000a and 2000b.
21. Alba, Logan, and Bellair 1994.
22. Although currently hindered by data limitations, others, in the future, might try to match predominantly African-American and Latino communities in similar cities, regress their homicide rates on a set of traditional control and independent variables (e.g., poverty and family structure), then explore the rates. This would allow comparisons of expected and predicted rates and seeing if the actual rates were significantly higher or lower. I thank Ralph Taylor for this suggestion.
23. For example, see Warner and Rountree 1997.
24. Cited in Butcher and Piehl 1998: 457.
25. Cohen et al. 1998.

FACT OR FICTION?

1. This paragraph, in part, also borrows from the account by Nevins 2002: 172.
2. See Russell 1998 for more on racial myths and hoaxes.
3. DiIulio, Bennett, and Walters 1996; Fox 1996.
4. Rodriguez 1998.
5. See Clara Rodriguez's introduction in her 1997 edited book.

6. Again, see Clara Rodriguez 1997: 180–83.

7. Rodriguez 1997.

8. Data on homicides, 1980–95, have been gathered directly from files in the Homicide Investigations Units of the El Paso, Miami, and San Diego Police Departments. I collected information on each homicide event, including location and circumstances surrounding each killing. Also included in the annual homicide "logs" and case-specific supplemental reports were extensive data on victim, and when known, offender characteristics such as age, gender, and ethnicity (White, Black, Latino, Haitian, or Asian). The logs and reports were copied, shipped to our home institution, read and coded by trained research assistants, and reviewed by the author.

9. Inciardi 1992.

10. These data are superior to the commonly used supplemental homicide reports (SHR) in detail, completeness, accuracy, and investigator control. As but one example, an advantage of the homicide files is the detailed individual-level information on each reported homicide. A separate category is provided for Latinos, allowing a distinction beyond the traditional categories of White and Black. Specific data on Latinos and other groups are lost once it is forwarded to the FBI's Uniform Crime Reports, so direct access to homicide files is essential. To calculate community-level counts and rates we focus attention on victim-level rather than offender data because information on offender ethnicity is less complete than for victims.

11. Direct access to circumstance or motive data was not completely available from the internal City of Houston supplemental homicide files in the early 1980s or for 1995. In the case of table 7.2, I relied on the 1980 to 1984 Uniform Crime Reports supplemental homicide records. In this specific instance, the UCR ethnicity and circumstance categories were relatively complete. I should also note that when these graphs were originally produced, the 1995 motive data in El Paso and Chicago were not readily available and the respective graphs reflect those missing records.

12. Cohen et al. 1998: 243

13. Blumstein 1995.

14. Cohen 1998: 244.

15. Ibid.: 245.

16. Blumstein 1995.

17. See, for example, Moore and Pinderhughes 1993, Escobar 1999, Sanders 1994, and Vigil 1987.

18. See Martinez and Lee 1999 for coding features.

19. Cohen et al. 1998; see also Anderson 1999 for a similar perspective.

20. See Fox and Zawitz 1999.

21. See Inciardi 1992; Inciardi, Horowitz, and Pottieger 1993.

22. Inciardi 1992.

23. Riedel and Best 1998.

24. Ibid.

25. Cook 1993; Sullivan 1989.

26. Short 1997.

27. Menjivar 2000: 231.

28. Escobar 1999: 203.

29. Inciardi and colleagues 1993: 115.

30. Portes and Stepick 1993.

31. Martinez, Lee, and Nielsen 2001: 38.

32. Martinez and Lee 2000.

33. Rodriguez 1993 provides occupational data.

34. See Anderson 1999 for parallel consequences.

CONCLUSION

1. Work on the ecology of crime has grown since Shaw and McKay, with recent sophisticated analyses of urban structure by Gottdiener 1994 and Taylor 2001.

2. For example, the growth of manufacturing, population expansion, etc.

3. Wilson 1987; 1996.

4. Abbott 1936; Du Bois 1899; Shaw and McKay 1931; 1969.

5. This is not to say that all analysts have focused exclusively on Black versus White comparisons. Some, such as Richard Alba, Mary Waters, Alejandro Portes, and others have started to decompose within and between ethnic group impacts extensively (see Alba et al. 1993; Alba, Logan, and Bellair 1994). But when it comes to the study of homicide and the ecology of violent crime overall, criminologists have fallen short of other social scientists in ethnic comparisons and have not yet established more sophistication in terms of ethnic group distinctions.

6. Gonzalez 2000; Moore and Pinderhughes 1993; Suro 1998; Suarez-Orozco 1998.

7. Again, I do not suggest that non-Latino immigrant groups are not making contributions to ethnic diversity or immigration research. Asians have increased in size in many West Coast cities, and Afro-Caribbean groups are growing along the East Coast corridor (Portes and Rumbaut 2001). The Latino immigration volume, in terms of size and scope, dwarfs that of all other ethnic groups.

8. See, for example, Hernandez-Leon and Zuniga 2001.

9. Short 1997: 204.

10. See Escobar 2000; Montejano 1986.

11. Anderson 1999.

12. For example, poverty relative to the home country.

13. Again, job attachments facilitated by institutions and social capital.
14. In fact, this finding is linked to Merton 1968: Latinos are more likely than similarly situated natives (i.e., African Americans) to have job opportunities (means) and lower expectations (goals).
15. Such as job training programs, education, public transportation, and professional occupation networks.
16. I am not suggesting that continuing to toil in poorly paid jobs is the correct or complete answer to future Latino success. Not only is it not a viable alternative to upward mobility, it also is a dangerous field for Latinos. Latino workplace injuries and deaths resulting from low-end jobs are on the rise and Latino death rates in this area are far greater than for Blacks and Whites (*New York Times,* July 16, 2001).
17. Menjivar 2000; Suro 1998.
18. Steinberg 1989.
19. Portes and Rumbaut (2001: 44–68) provide an exceptional essay on the current barriers facing immigrant absorption into mainstream America (for more historical perspective see Steinberg 1989).
20. See Portes and Rumbaut 2001; Steinberg 1989 provides a historical perspective.
21. Menjivar 2000; Portes 2000; Waldinger 1996.
22. Lieberson 1980; Menjivar 2000; Waldinger 1996.
23. Here I refer to the use of "social capital," loosely defined as the ability to generate resources to exchange with others through informal exchanges, in turn creating stronger ties and networks that help deflect crime (see Portes 1995; Menjivar 2000 provides a different take in the case of immigrant Salvadorans).
24. Waters 1999.
25. Menjivar 2000: 222.
26. Ibid.: 233.
27. Lee, Martinez, and Rodriguez 2000.
28. See Pedraza-Bailey 1985.
29. The increased number of Border Police and the use of terminology such as the "War on Drugs" or "fighting to hold the line" at the U.S./Mexico border are conspicuous examples of moral panics and, to an extent, the encouragement of official violence. These metaphors help create a warlike image designed to stem the influx of aliens and drug carriers, thereby protecting our borders. To the extent that warlike conditions and official violence legitimize the general use of violence in society, we should expect high crime rates on the border over and above other ingredients of urban violence (Valdez 1993). Yet they are not apparent in our analysis.
30. Sassen 1988; 1991: Massey and Espinosa 1997.
31. See Portes 1996.
32. Lane 1986; 1997.

33. It may be worth mentioning findings relative to Little Haiti—the one exception where immigration into a Black area did occur and resulted in suppressed homicide rates (see Martinez and Lee 2000a).
34. Scalia 1996.
35. Menjivar 2000: 241–43.
36. Taken to its logical conclusion, this suggests that business owners benefit both from anti-immigrant sentiment and the illegal status of one class of immigrants, since vulnerabilities provide opportunities for exploitation. This implies that current policies are fundamentally rooted in the political economy, and therefore these policy suggestions will likely encounter opposition for this and other reasons.
37. For research on the "costs" of legal versus illegal arrestees in primarily property and misdemeanor offenses see Pennell, Curtis, and Tayman 1989. However, there has been little if any systematic research suggesting overinvolvement of illegals in violent crime.
38. For example, roofing, trench digging, carrying heavy materials, etc.
39. Waldinger 1996.
40. Wilson 1996.
41. Steffensmeier and Demuth 2001: 725.
42. Osgood and Chambers 2000.
43. *New York Times,* April 2, 2001.

REFERENCES

Abbott, Edith. *The Tenements of Chicago 1908–1935.* Chicago: University of Chicago Press, 1936.

Abbott, Grace. "Immigration and Crime." *Journal of Criminal Law and Criminology* 6 (1915): 522–32.

Acuna, Rodolfo. *Occupied America: A History of Chicanos,* 4th ed. New York: Longman, 2000.

Aguirre, Benigno E., Rogelio Saenz, and Brian Sinclair James. "Marielitos Ten Years Later: The Scarface Legacy." *Social Science Quarterly* 78 (1997): 487–507.

Alaniz, Maria L., Randi S. Cartmill, and Robert N. Parker. "Immigrants and Violence: The Importance of Neighborhood Context." *Hispanic Journal of Behavioral Sciences* 20 (1998): 155–74.

Alba, Richard D., John R. Logan, and Paul E. Bellair. "Living with Crime: The Implications of Racial/Ethnic Differences in Suburban Location." *Social Forces* 73 (1994): 395–434.

American Friends Service Committee. *Abuse Report 2000: Complaints of Abuse on the U.S. Mexico Border and in the San Diego Region by Local and Federal Law Enforcement Agencies.* Retrieved March 23, 2001 from the World Wide Web: *http://www.afsc.org/border00.htm,* 2000.

Anderson, Elijah. *Streetwise: Race, Class, and Change in an Urban Community.* Chicago: University of Chicago Press, 1990.

———. *Code of the Street.* New York: W. W. Norton, 1999.

Bankston, Carl L. III. "Youth Gangs and the New Second Generation: A Review Essay." *Aggression and Violent Behavior* 3 (1998): 35–45.

Bean, Frank, and Marta Tienda. *The Hispanic Population of the United States.* New York: Russell Sage Foundation, 1987.

Beasley, Ronald W., and George Antunes. "The Etiology of Urban Crime: An Ecological Analysis." *Criminology* 22 (1974): 531–50.

Beck, Roy. *The Case against Immigration.* New York: W. W. Norton, 1996.

Betancur, John J. "Settlement Experiences of Latinos in Chicago: Segregation, Speculation, and the Ecology Model." *Social Forces* 74 (1996): 1299–1324.

Block, Carolyn R. "Race/Ethnicity and Patterns of Chicago Homicide, 1965–1981." *Crime & Delinquency* 31 (1985): 104–16.

Block, Carolyn R., Richard L. Block, and the Illinois Criminal Justice Information Authority. *Homicide in Chicago, 1965–1995,* 4th ICPSR version. Chicago: Illinois Criminal Justice Information Auhtority, 1998; Ann Arbor, Mich.: ICPSR, 1998.

Blumstein, Alfred. "Youth Violence, Guns, and the Illicit-Drug Industry." *Journal of Criminology and Criminal Law* 86 (1995): 10–36.

Bowler, Alida C. "Recent Statistics on Crime and the Foreign Born." In National Commission on Law Observance and Enforcement, *Report on Crime and the Foreign-Born.* Washington, D.C.: U.S. Government Printing Office, 1931.

Bradshaw, Benjamin, et al. "A Historical Geographical Study of Lethal Violence in San Antonio." *Social Science Quarterly* 79 (1998): 863–78.

Brimelow, Peter J. *Alien Nation.* New York: Random House, 1995.

Bullock, Henry A. "Urban Homicide in Theory and Fact." *Journal of Criminal Law, Criminology, and Police Sciences* 45 (1955): 565–75.

Bursik, Robert J. "Social Disorganization and Theories of Crime and Delinquency: Problems and Prospects." *Criminology* 56 (1988): 519–51.

Butcher, Kristin F., and Anne Morrison Piehl. "Cross-City Evidence on the Relationship between Immigration and Crime." *Journal of Policy Analysis and Management* 17 (1998): 457–93.

Camarillo, Albert. *Chicanos in a Changing Society: From Mexican Pueblos to American Barrios in Santa Barbara and Southern California, 1848–1930*. Cambridge, Mass.: Harvard University Press, 1979.

Camarota, Steve A. "The Wages of Immigration: The Effect on the Low-Skilled Labor Market." Washington, D.C.: Center for Immigration Studies Center Paper 12, 1998.

Castro, Diego O. "Stereotyping by the Media." In *Images of Color, Images of Crime,* edited by C. R. Mann and M. S. Zatz. Los Angeles: Roxbury, 1998.

Chin, Ko-Lin. *Chinese Subculture and Criminality: Non-Traditional Crime Groups in America*. Westport, Conn.: Greenwood Press, 1990.

Cohen, Jacqueline, et al. "The Role of Drug Markets and Gangs in Local Homicide Rates." *Homicide Studies* 2 (1998): 241–62.

Cook, Phillip J. "Notes on the Availability and Prevalence of Firearms." *American Journal of Preventive Medicine* 9 (1993): 33–38.

Cook, Phillip J., and John Laub. "The Unprecedented Epidemic in Youth Violence." In *Youth Violence,* edited by M. Tonry and M. H. Moore. Chicago: University of Chicago Press, 1998.

Council of Economic Advisers for the President's Initiative on Race. *Changing America: Indicators of Social and Economic Well-Being by Race and Hispanic Origin*. http://w3.access.gpo.gov/eop/ca/index.html, 1999.

De la Garza, Rodolfo, et al. *Latino Voices: Mexican, Puerto Rican, & Cuban Perspectives on American Politics.* Boulder, Colo.: Westview Press, 1992.

DiIulio, John, William J. Bennett, and John P. Walters. *Body Count: Moral Poverty—and How to Win America's War against Crime and Drugs.* New York: Simon & Schuster, 1996.

Du Bois, W. E. B. *The Philadelphia Negro: A Social Study.* 1899. Reprint, New York: Schocken Books, 1967.

Dunn, Marvin. *Black Miami in the Twentieth Century.* Gainesville, Fla.: University Press of Florida, 1997.

Du Phuoc Long, Patrick. *The Dream Shattered: Vietnamese Gangs in America.* Boston: Northeastern University Press, 1996.

Eschbach, Karl, Jacqueline Hagan, Nestor Rodriguez, Ruben Hernandez Leon, and Stanley Bailey. "Death at the Border." *International Migration Review* 33 (1999): 430–54.

Escobar, Edward J. *Race, Police, and the Making of a Political Identity: Mexican Americans and the Los Angeles Police Department, 1900–1945.* Berkeley: University of California Press, 1999.

Ferracuti, Franco. "European Migration and Crime." In *Crime and Culture: Essays in Honor of Thorsten Sellin,* edited by M. Wolfgang. New York: John Wiley & Sons, 1968.

Fox, James Alan. *Trends in Juvenile Violence: A Report to the United States Attorney General on Current and Future Rates of Juvenile Offending.* Washington, D.C.: Bureau of Justice Statistics, 1996.

Fox, James Alan, and Marianne W. Zawitz. "Homicide Trends in the United States." *Bureau of Justice Statistics Crime Data Brief.* Washington, D.C.: U.S. Department of Justice Office of Justice Programs, 1999.

Gans, Herbert J. "Second Generation Decline: Scenarios for the Economic and Ethnic Futures of the post-1965 American Immigrants." *Ethnic and Racial Studies* 15 (1992): 173–92.

Garcia, Maria C. *Havana USA: Cuban Exiles and Cuban Americans in South Florida, 1959–1994.* Berkeley: University of California Press, 1996.

Garcia, Mario T. *Desert Immigrant: The Mexicans of El Paso, 1880–1920.* New Haven, Conn.: Yale University Press, 1981.

Gonzalez, Juan. *A History of Latinos in America: Harvest of Empire.* New York: Viking Press, 2000.

Gottdiener, Mark. *The Social Production of Urban Space,* 2nd ed. Austin: University of Texas Press, 1994.

Grenier, Guillermo, and Lisandro Perez. "Miami Spice: The Ethnic Cauldron Simmers." In *Origins and Destinies,* edited by S. Pedraza and R. G. Rumbaut. Belmont, Calif.: Wadsworth, 1996.

Gurr, Ted R. "The History of Violent Crime in America." In *Violence in America,* vol. 1, edited by T. R. Gurr. Newbury Park, Calif.: Sage, 1989.

Gutierrez, David. *Walls and Mirrors: Mexican Americans, Mexican Immigrants, and the Politics of Ethnicity.* Berkeley: University of California Press, 1995.

Hagan, Jacqueline. *Deciding to Be Legal: A Maya Community in Houston.* Philadelphia: Temple University Press, 1994.

Hagan, John, and Alberto Palloni. "Immigration and Crime in the United States." In *The Immigration Debate,* edited by J. P. Smith and B. Edmonston. Washington, D.C.: National Academy Press, 1998.

Handlin, Oscar. *The American People in the Twentieth Century.* Cambridge, Mass.: Harvard University Press, 1954.

————. *The Newcomers: Negroes and Puerto Ricans in A Changing Metropolis.* Cambridge, Mass.: Harvard University Press, 1959.

Hawkins, Darnell F. "African Americans and Homicide." In *Issues in the Study and Prevention of Homicide,* edited by M. D. Smith and M. Zahn. Newbury Park, Calif.: Sage, 1999.

Hernandez-Leon, Ruben, and Victor Zuniga. "Making Carpet by the Mile": The Emergence of a Mexican Immigrant Community in an Industrial Region of the U.S. Historic South." *Social Science Quarterly* 81 (2000): 49–66.

Herzog, Lawrence A. *Where North Meets South: Cities, Space, and Politics on the U.S.–Mexico Border.* Austin, Tex.: Center for Mexican-American Studies, 1990.

Holmes, Steven A. "For Hispanic Poor, No Silver Lining." *New York Times* (October 13, 1996).

Immigration and Naturalization Service. *Statistical Yearbook of the Immigration and Naturalization Service,* 1986. Washington, D.C.: U.S. Government Printing Office, 1987.

Immigration and Naturalization Service. *Statistical Yearbook of the Immigration and Naturalization Service,* 1996. Washington, D.C.: U.S. Government Printing Office, 1997.

Inciardi, James A. The War on Drugs II. Mountain View, Calif.: Mayfield, 1992.

Inciardi, James A., Anne E. Pottieger, and Ruth Horowitz. *Street Kids, Street Drugs, Street Crime: An Examination of Drug Use and Serious Delinquency in Miami.* Belmont, Calif.: Wadsworth, 1993.

Jackall, Robert. 1997. *Wild Cowboys: Urban Marauders & the Forces of Order.* Cambridge, Mass.: Harvard University Press.

Jonassen, Christen T. "A Reevaluation and Critique of the Logic and Some Methods of Shaw and McKay." *American Sociological Review* 14 (1949): 608–14.

Kennedy, David M. "Can We Still Afford to Be a Nation of Immigrants?" *Atlantic Monthly* (November 1996): 52–55, 68.

Kobrin, Solomon. "The Chicago Area Project: A 25-Year Assessment." *Annals, AAPSS* 322 (1959): 19–29.

LaFree, Gary. *Losing Legitimacy.* Boulder, Colo.: Westview Press, 1998.

Lamm, Richard D., and Gary Imhoff. *The Immigration Time Bomb.* New York: Truman Talley Books, 1985.

Lane, Roger. *Roots of Violence in Black Philadelphia 1860–1900.* Cambridge, Mass.: Harvard University Press, 1986.

———. *Murder in America: A History.* Columbus: Ohio State University Press, 1997.

Laughlin, Harry H. "Immigration and Conquest." New York: Special Committee on Immigration and Naturalization of the Chamber of Commerce of the State of New York, 1939.

Lee, Matthew T., Ramiro Martinez Jr., and S. Fernando Rodriguez. "Contrasting Latinos in Homicide Research: The Victim and Offender Relationship in El Paso and Miami." *Social Science Quarterly* 81 (2000): 375–88.

Lee, Matthew T., Ramiro Martinez Jr., and Richard Rosenfeld. "Does Immigration Increase Homicide Rates? Negative Evidence from Three Border Cities." *The Sociological Quarterly* 42 (2001): 559–580.

Lewis, Oscar. *La Vida: A Puerto Rican Family in the Culture of Poverty.* New York: Random House, 1965.

Leyba, Cynthia. "Homicides in Bernaillo County: 1978–1982." In *Research Conference on Violence and Homicide in Hispanic Communities Proceedings,* edited by J. F. Kraus, S. B. Sorenson, and P. D. Juarez. Washington, D.C.: U.S. Department of Health and Human Services, 1987.

Lieberson, Stanley. *A Piece of the Pie: Blacks and White Immigrants since 1980.* Berkeley: University of California Press, 1980.

Lind, Andrew W. "Some Ecological Patterns of Community Disorganization in Honolulu." *American Journal of Sociology* 36 (1930): 206–20.

Lollock, Lisa. *The Foreign-Born Population in the United States: March 2000.* Current Population Reports P20-534. Washington, D.C.: U.S. Census Bureau, 2001.

Mann, Coramae Richey. *Unequal Justice: A Question of Color.* Bloomington: Indiana University Press, 1993.

Martinez, Oscar J. *Border Boom Town.* Austin: University of Texas Press, 1975.

———. *Border People.* Tucson: University of Arizona Press, 1994.

Martinez, Ramiro Jr. "Latinos and Lethal Violence: The Impact of Poverty and Inequality." *Social Problems* 43 (1996): 131–46.

———. "Homicide among the 1980 Mariel Refugees in Miami: Victims and Offenders." *Hispanic Journal of Behavioral Sciences* 19 (1997): 107–22.

Martinez, Ramiro Jr., and Matthew T. Lee. "Immigration and the Ethnic Distribution of Homicide in Miami, 1985–1995." *Homicide Studies* 2 (1998): 291–304.

———. "Extending Ethnicity in Homicide Research: The Case of Latinos." In *Homicide: A Sourcebook of Social Research*, edited by M. D. Smith and M. Zahn. Newbury Park, Calif.: Sage, 1999.

———. "Comparing the Context of Immigrant Homicides in Miami: Haitians, Jamaicans, and Mariels." *International Migration Review* 34 (2000a): 794–812.

———. "Immigration and Crime." In *National Institute of Justice Criminal Justice 2000: The Nature of Crime: Continuity and Change,* vol. 1, edited by Gary LaFree, Robert J. Bursik Jr., James F. Short Jr., and Ralph B. Taylor. Washington, D.C.: National Institute of Justice, 2000b.

Martinez, Ramiro Jr., Matthew T. Lee, and Amie L. Nielsen. "Revisiting the Scarface Legacy: The Victim/Offender Relationship and Mariel Homicides in Miami." *Hispanic Journal of Behavioral Sciences,* February (2001): 37–56.

Massey, Douglas. "Latinos, Poverty, and the Underclass: A New Agenda for Research." *Hispanic Journal of Behavioral Sciences* 15 (1993): 449–75.

Massey, Douglas, and Nancy Denton. "Hypersegregation in U.S. Metropolitan Areas: Black and White Segregation along Five Dimensions." *Demography* 26 (1989): 373–91.

Massey, Douglas, and Kristin E. Espinoza. "What's Driving Mexico–U.S. Migration? A Theoretical, Empirical, and Policy Analysis." *American Journal of Sociology* 102 (1997): 939–99.

Mata, Alberto G. "Stereotyping by Politicians." In *Images of Color, Images of Crime,* edited by C. R. Mann and M. S. Zatz. Los Angeles: Roxbury, 1998.

Mazon, Mauricio. *The Zoot-Suit Riots.* Austin, Tex.: Center for Mexican-American Studies, 1984.

McCord, Joan. "Ethnicity, Acculturation, and Opportunities: A Study of Two Generations." In *Ethnicity, Race, and Crime,* edited by D. F. Hawkins. Albany: State University of New York Press, 1995.

McKanna, Clare V. *Homicide, Race, and Justice in the American West, 1880–1920.* Tucson: University of Arizona Press, 1997.

McWilliams, Carey. *North from Mexico: The Spanish-Speaking People of the United States.* 1948. Reprint, New York: Greenwood Press, 1968.

Menjivar, Cecilia. *Fragmented Ties: Salvadoran Immigrant Networks in America.* Berkeley: University of California Press, 2000.

Merton, Robert K. "Social Structure and Anomie." *American Sociological Review* 3 (1938): 672–82.

Miles, Jack. "Blacks versus Browns: The Struggle for the Bottom Rung." *Atlantic Monthly* (October 1992), pp. 52–55, 58.

Miller, Jerome G. *Search and Destroy: African-American Males in the Criminal Justice System.* New York: Cambridge University Press, 1996.

Mladenka, K. R., and K. Q. Hill. "A Reexamination of the Etiology of Urban Crime." *Criminology* 13 (1976): 491–506.

Monkkonen, Eric H. "Diverging Homicide Rates: England and the United States, 1850–1875." In *Violence in America,* vol. 1, edited by T. R. Gurr. Newbury Park, Calif.: Sage, 1989.

———. *Murder in New York City.* Berkeley: University of California Press, 2001.

Montejano, David. *Anglos and Mexicans in the Making of Texas, 1836–1986.* Austin: University of Texas Press, 1987.

———. "On the Question of Inclusion." In *Chicano Politics and Society in the Late Twentieth Century,* edited by D. Montejano. Austin: University of Texas Press, 1999.

Moore, Joan, and Harry Pachon. *Hispanics in the United States*. Englewood Cliffs, N.J.: Prentice-Hall, 1985.

Moore, Joan, and Raquel Pinderhughes. "Introduction." In *In the Barrios: Latinos and the Underclass Debate*, edited by J. Moore and R. Pinderhughes. New York: Russell Sage Foundation, 1993.

Muller, Thomas. *Immigrants and the American City*. New York: New York University Press, 1993.

National Commission on Law Observance and Enforcement. *Report on Crime and the Foreign-Born*. Washington, D.C.: U.S. Government Printing Office, 1931.

Nelsen, Candice, Jay Corzine, and Lin-Huff Corzine. "The Violent West Reexamined: A Research Note on Regional Homicide Rates." *Criminology* 32 (1994): 149–61.

Nevins, Joseph. *Operation Gatekeeper: The Rise of the "Illegal Alien" and the Making of the U.S.–Mexico Boundary*. New York: Routledge, 2002.

New York Times. "Many Hispanics Entering Small Towns, Census Reports" (April 2, 2001).

Oboler, Suzanne. *Ethnic Labels, Latino Lives*. Minneapolis: University of Minnesota Press, 1995.

Osgood, Wayne D., and Jeff M. Chambers. "Social Disorganization outside the Metropolis: An Analysis of Rural Youth Violence." *Criminology* 38 (2000): 81–116.

Ousey, Graham. "Homicide, Structural Factors, and the Racial Invariance Assumption." *Criminology* 37 (1999): 405–26.

Padilla, Amado M. "The Role of Cultural Awareness and Ethnic Royalty in Acculturation." In *Acculturation: Theory, Models, and Some New*

Findings, edited by A. M. Padilla. Boulder, Colo.: Westview Press, 1980.

Padilla, Elena. *Puerto Rican Immigration in New York and Chicago.* Ph.D. diss., University of Chicago, 1947.

Padilla, Felix. *Puerto Rican Chicago.* Notre Dame, Ind.: University of Notre Dame Press, 1987.

———. "The Quest for Community: Puerto Ricans in Chicago." In *In the Barrios: Latinos and the Underclass Debate,* edited by J. Moore and R. Pinderhughes. New York: Russell Sage Foundation, 1993.

Parker, Robert N. *Alcohol and Homicide: A Deadly Combination of Two American Traditions.* Albany: State University of New York Press, 1995.

Patricios, Nicholas N. *Building Marvelous Miami.* Gainesville: University Press of Florida, 1994.

Pedraza, Silvia. "Cuba's Refugees: Manifold Migrations." In *Origins and Destinies,* edited by S. Pedraza and R. G. Rumbaut. Belmont, Calif.: Wadsworth, 1996.

Pedraza-Bailey, Silvia. *Political and Economic Migrants in America: Cubans and Mexicans.* Austin: University of Texas Press, 1985.

Pennell, Susan, Christine Curtis, and Jeff Tayman. *The Impact of Illegal Immigration on the Criminal Justice System.* San Diego, Calif.: San Diego Association of Governments, 1989.

Pokorny, Alex. "Human Violence: A Comparison of Homicide, Aggravated Assault, Suicide, and Attempted Suicide." *Journal of Criminal Law, Criminology, and Police Science* 56 (1965): 488–97.

Portes, Alejandro. "The Social Origins of the Cuban Enclave Economy of Miami." *Sociological Perspectives* 30 (1987): 476–85.

———. *The New Second Generation*. New York: Russell Sage Foundation, 1996.

Portes, Alejandro, and Robert L. Bach. *Latin Journey*. Berkeley: University of California Press, 1985.

Portes, Alejandro, and Ruben G. Rumbaut. *Immigrant America*. Berkeley: University of California Press, 1990.

———. *Immigrant America*, 2nd ed. Berkeley: University of California Press, 1996.

Portes, Alejandro, and Alex Stepick. *City on the Edge: The Transformation of Miami*. Berkeley: University of California Press, 1993.

Portes, Alejandro and Ruben G. Rumbaut. *Legacies: The Story of the Immigrant Second Generation*. Berkeley: University of California Press, 2001.

Portillos, Edwardo L. "Images of Crime and Punishment." In *Images of Color, Images of Crime*, edited by C. R. Mann and M. S. Zatz. Los Angeles: Roxbury, 1998.

Reidel, Marc, and Joel Best. "Patterns in Intimate Partner Homicide: California, 1987–1996." *Homicide Studies* 2 (1998): 305–20.

Reiss, Albert J. Jr., and Jeffery A. Roth, eds. *Understanding and Preventing Violence*. Washington, D.C.: National Academy Press, 1993.

Rodriguez, Clara E. *Puerto Ricans: Born in the U.S.A.* Boston: Unwim Hyman, 1989.

———. "Keeping It Reel? Films of the 1980s and 1990s." In *Images of Latinas and Latinos in the U.S. Media*. Boulder, Colo.: Westview Press, 1997.

Rodriguez, Luis. "Images of Latinos and Latinas." In *Images of Color,*

Images of Crime, edited by C. R. Mann and M. S. Zatz. Los Angeles: Roxbury, 1998.

Rodriguez, Nestor P. "Economic Restructuring and Latino Growth in Houston." In *In the Barrios: Latinos and the Underclass Debate,* edited by Joan Moore and Raquel Pinderhughes. New York: Russell Sage Foundation, 1993.

Romo, Ricardo. *East Los Angeles: A History of a Barrio.* Austin: University of Texas Press, 1983.

Roper Reports. *Roper Report 95–4.* New York: Roper Starch Worldwide, 1995.

Rosenwaike, Ira, and Katherine Hempstead. "Mortality among Three Puerto Rican Populations: Residents of Puerto Rico and Migrants in New York City and in the Balance of the United States, 1979–81." *International Migration Review* 24 (1990): 684–702.

Ross, Harold. "Crime and the Native-Born Sons of European Immigrants." *Journal of Criminal Law and Criminology* 28 (1937): 202–9.

Rumbaut, Ruben G. *Immigrants from Latinos and the Caribbean: A Socioeconomic Profile.* CIFFRAS no. 6, Julian Samora Research Institute. East Lansing, Mich.: Michigan State University, 1995.

Russell, Katheryn. *The Color of Crime.* New York: New York University Press, 1998.

Sampson, Robert, and Janet L. Lauritsen. "Racial and Ethnic Disparities in Crime and Criminal Justice in the United States," In *Ethnicity, Crime, and Immigration,* edited by M. Tonry. Chicago: University of Chicago Press, 1997.

Sampson, Robert J., and William Julius Wilson. "Toward a Theory of Race, Crime, and Urban Inequality." In *Crime and Inequality,* edited by J. Hagan and R. Peterson. Stanford, Calif.: Stanford University Press, 1995.

Sanchez, George J. *Becoming Mexican American: Ethnicity, Culture and Identity in Chicano Los Angeles, 1900–1945.* New York: Oxford University Press, 1993.

Sanchez, Reymundo. *My Bloody Life: The Making of a Latin King.* Chicago: Chicago Review Press, 2000.

Sanchez-Jankowski, Martin. *Islands in the Street: Gangs and American Urban Society.* Berkeley: University of California Press, 1991.

Sanders, William B. *Gangbangs and Drive-bys.* Hawthorne, N.Y.: Aldine de Gruyter, 1994.

Santoro, Wayne A. "Conventional Politics Takes Center Stage: The Latino Struggle against English-Only Laws." *Social Forces* 77 (1999) 887–910.

Sassen, Saskia. *The Mobility of Labor and Capital.* Cambridge, Eng.: Cambridge University Press, 1988.

———. *The Global City: New York, London, Tokyo.* Princeton, N.J.: Princeton University Press, 1991

Scalia, John. *Noncitizens in the Federal Criminal Justice System, 1984–1994.* Washington, D.C.: U.S. Department of Justice, Bureau of Justice Statistics, 1996.

Schmitt, Eric. "Census Figures Show Hispanics Pulling Even with Blacks." *New York Times* (March 8, 2001).

Sellin, Thorsten. *Culture Conflict and Crime.* New York: Social Science Research Council, 1938.

Shaw, Clifford R., and Henry D. McKay. *Social Factors in Juvenile Delinquency.* Vol. II of Report on the Causes of Crime. National Commission on Law Observance and Enforcement, Report no. 13. Washington, D.C.: U.S. Government Printing Office, 1931.

———. *Juvenile Delinquency and Urban Areas.* 1942. Reprint, Chicago: University of Chicago Press, 1969.

Short, James F. *Poverty, Ethnicity, and Violent Crime.* Boulder, Colo.: Westview Press, 1997.

Simon, Rita J. *Public Opinion and the Immigrant: Print Media Coverage, 1880–1980.* Lexington, Mass.: Lexington Books, 1985.

———. "Immigration and American Attitudes." *Public Opinion* 10 (1987): 47–50.

Skerry, Peter. *Mexican Americans: The Ambivalent Minority.* New York: Free Press, 1993.

Spence, Richard. "A Hispanic Homicide Risk Model for Border Areas." In *Research Conference on Violence and Homicide in Hispanic Communities Proceedings,* edited by J. F. Kraus, S. B. Sorenson, and P. D. Juarez. Washington, D.C.: U.S. Department of Health and Human Services, 1987.

Steffensmeier, Darrell, and Stephen Demuth. "Ethnicity and Judges' Sentencing Decisions: Hispanic-Black-White Comparisons." *Criminology* 39 (2001): 145–78.

Steinberg, Stephen. *The Ethnic Myth.* Boston: Beacon Press, 1989.

Stepick, Alex, and Guillermo Grenier. "Cubans in Miami." In *In the Barrios: Latinos and the Underclass Debate,* edited by J. Moore and R. Pinderhughes. New York: Russell Sage Foundation, 1993.

Suarez-Orozco, Marcelo M. "Introduction." In *Crossings: Mexican Immigration in Interdisciplinary Perspectives,* edited by M. M. Suarez-Orozco. Cambridge, Mass.: Harvard University Press, 1998.

Sullivan, Mercer. *"Getting Paid": Youth Crime and Work in the Inner City.* Ithaca, N.Y.: Cornell University Press, 1989.

Suro, Roberto. *Strangers among US: How Latino Immigration Is Transforming America*. New York: Alfred A. Knopf, 1998.

Sutherland, Edwin H. *Principles of Criminology*. Philadelphia: J. B. Lippincott, 1934.

————. *Principles of Criminology,* 4th ed. Philadelphia: J. B. Lippincott, 1947.

Sutherland, Edwin H., and Donald R. Cressey. *Principles of Criminology*. Philadelphia: J. B. Lippincott, 1960.

Taft, Donald R. "Nationality and Crime." *American Sociological Review* 1 (1936): 724–36.

Tanton, John, and Wayne Lutton. "Immigration and Criminality in the U.S.A." *Journal of Social, Political, and Economic Studies* 18 (1993): 217–34.

Taylor, Paul S. "Crime and the Foreign-Born: The Problem of the Mexican." In National Commission on Law Observance and Enforcement, *Report on Crime and the Foreign-Born*. Washington, D.C.: U.S. Government Printing Office, 1931.

————. *Mexican Labor in the United States: Chicago and the Calumet Region*. Berkeley: University of California Publications in Economics, 1932.

————. *An American-Mexican Frontier*. Chapel Hill: University of North Carolina Press, 1934.

Taylor, Ralph. *Breaking Away from Broken Windows: Baltimore Neighborhoods and the Nationwide Fight against Crime, Grime, Fear, and Decline*. Boulder, Colo.: Westview Press, 2001.

Thomas, William I., and Florian Znaniecki. *The Polish Peasant in Europe and America*. Vol. IV, *Disorganization and Reorganization in Poland*. Boston: Gorham Press, 1918–20.

————. 1918–20. *The Polish Peasant in Europe and America,* edited and abridged. Reprint, Champaign: University of Illinois Press, 1984.

Thrasher, Frederic. *The Gang: A Study of 1,313 Gangs in Chicago.* Chicago: University of Chicago Press, 1927.

Tonry, Michael. "Ethnicity, Crime, and Immigration." In *Ethnicity, Crime, and Immigration,* edited by M. Tonry. Chicago: University of Chicago Press, 1997.

U.S. Bureau of the Census. *1990 Census of Population and Housing: Summary Tape File 3A.* Retrieved March 30, 2000, from the World Wide Web: http://venus.census.gov/cdrom/lookup.

U.S. Bureau of the Census. *Hispanic Population of the United States Current Population Survey—March 1995.* Washington, D.C.: U.S. Bureau of the Census, Population Division, Ethnic & Hispanic Statistics Branch, 1995.

U.S. Commission on Immigration Reform. *Restoring Credibility.* Washington, D.C.: U.S. Commission on Immigration Reform, 1994.

Valdez, Avelardo. "Persistent Poverty, Crime, and Drugs: U.S.-Mexican Border Region." In *In the Barrios: Latinos and the Underclass Debate,* edited by J. Moore and R. Hinderhughes. New York: Russell Sage Foundation, 1993.

Valdez, R. Burciaga, and Parivash Nourjah. "Homicide in Southern California, 1966–1985: An Examination Based on Vital Statistics Data." In *Research Conference on Violence and Homicide in Hispanic Communities Proceedings,* edited by J. F. Kraus, S. B. Sorenson, and P. D. Juarez. Washington, D.C.: U.S. Department of Health and Human Services, 1987.

Velez-Ibañez, Carlos. "U.S. Mexicans in the Borderlands: Being Poor without the Underclass." In *In the Barrios: Latinos and the Underclass Debate,* edited by J. Moore and R. Hinderhughes. New York: Russell Sage Foundation, 1993.

Vigil, James D. *From Indians to Chicanos: The Dynamics of Mexican-American Culture.* Prospect Heights, Ill.: Waveland Press, 1980.

———. "Street Socialization, Locura Behavior, and Violence among Chicano Gang Members." In *Research Conference on Violence and Homicide in Hispanic Communities Proceedings,* edited by J. F. Kraus, S. B. Sorenson, and P. D. Juarez. Washington, D.C.: U.S. Department of Health and Human Services, 1987.

———. *From Indians to Chicanos: The Dynamics of Mexican-American Culture,* 2nd ed. Prospect Heights, Ill.: Waveland Press, 1998.

Vigil, James D., and J. M. Long. "Emic and Etic Perspectives on Gang Culture: The Chicano Case." In *Gangs in America,* edited by C. R. Huff. Newbury Park, Calif.: Sage, 1990.

Waldinger, Roger. *Still the Promised Land?* Cambridge, Mass.: Harvard University Press, 1996.

Warner, Barbara D., and Pamela W. Rountree. "Local Social Ties in a Community and Crime Model: Questioning the Systemic Nature of Informal Social Control." *Social Problems* (1997) 44: 520–36.

Waters, Tony. *Crime and Immigrant Youth.* Thousand Oaks, Calif.: Sage, 1999.

Webb, Walter Prescott. *The Texas Rangers: A Century of Frontier Defense.* Austin: University of Texas Press, 1965.

Wilbanks, William. *Murder in Miami: An Analysis of Homicide Patterns and Trends in Dade County (Miami) Florida, 1917–1983.* Lanham, Md.: University Press of America, 1984.

Wilson, James Q. "Crime, Race, and Values." *Society* (November–December 1992): 90–93.

Wilson, William J. *The Truly Disadvantaged.* Chicago: University of Chicago Press, 1987.

————. *When Work Disappears*. New York: Alfred A. Knopf, 1996.

Wolfgang, Marvin, and Franco Ferracuti. *The Subculture of Violence: Towards an Integrated Theory in Criminology*. London: Tavistock, 1967.

Wolfgang, Marvin E. *Patterns in Criminal Homicide*. Philadelphia: University of Pennsylvania Press, 1958.

Woll, Allen L. "Hollywood Bandits, 1910–1981." In *Bandidos: The Varieties of Latin American Banditry*, edited by Richard W. Slatta. New York: Greenwood Press, 1987.

Yeager, Matthew G. "Immigrants and Criminality: A Review." *Criminal Justice Abstracts* 29 (1997): 143–71.

Young, Pauline V. "Social Problems in the Education of the Immigrant Child." *American Sociological Review* 1 (1936): 419–29.

Zahn, Margaret. "Homicide in Nine American Cities: The Hispanic Case." In *Research Conference on Violence and Homicide in Hispanic Communities Proceedings,* edited by J. F. Kraus, S. B. Sorenson, and P. D. Juarez. Washington, D.C:. U.S. Department of Health and Human Services, 1987.

Zatz, Marjorie S., and Coramae Richey Mann. "The Power of Images." In *Images of Color, Images of Crime,* edited by C. R. Mann and M. S. Zatz. Los Angeles: Roxbury, 1998.

Zucker, Norman L., and Naomi F. Zucker. *Desperate Crossings: Seeking Refuge in America*. Armonk, N.Y.: M. E. Sharpe, 1996.

INDEX